THE EXPERIENCE MEETING

An Introduction to the Welsh Societies of the Evangelical Awakening

WILLIAM WILLIAMS

Translated by Mrs. Lloyd-Jones
with an introduction by Dr. D. Martyn Lloyd-Jones

REGENT COLLEGE PUBLISHING
Vancouver, British Columbia

First published jointly by Evangelical Press, London, annd Evangelical Movement of Wales, 1973.

This edition published 2003 by Regent College Publishing
5800 University Boulevard
Vancouver, BC V6T 2E4 Canada
www.regentpublishing.com

National Library of Canada Cataloguing in Publication Data

Williams, William, 1717-1791.
The experience meeting: an introduction to the Welsh societies of the Evangelical Awakening / William Williams; translated by Mrs. Lloyd Jones and including an introduction by Dr. D. Martyn Lloyd-Jones.

ISBN 1-57383-043-7 (United States)
ISBN 1-55361-074-1(Canada)

1. Religious gatherings—Welsh Calvinistic Methodist Church. 2. Evangelical Revival—Great Britain. 3. Calvinistic Methodists—Wales. I. Title.

BX9100.W54 2003 285'.235 C2003-910012-X

INTRODUCTION

THE Methodist or Evangelical Awakening of the 18th century began in Wales some two years before that in England, and was quite independent of it for a number of years. That they were part of the same movement of the Spirit of God is shown clearly by the many features that were common to both.

There was the same inspired, fervent, warm preaching, with great emphasis on repentance, justification, regeneration and assurance of salvation, the same itinerant ministry outside the bounds of the particular parishes of the preachers, and the open-air or field-preaching which attracted the masses who never attended the churches.

However, in many ways the most striking similarity was the way in which, independently of each other, the leaders were led to gather together the converts into little groups or societies for further teaching and nurturing in the Faith. These men of God had a great concern for the souls of the people, and realising that the parish churches were so spiritually dead that they could provide neither the fellowship nor the teaching that was necessary for these raw converts, they developed the idea of these 'religious societies' where such people could meet together regularly every week.

The object of the societies was primarily to provide a fellowship in which the new spiritual life and experience of the people could be safeguarded and developed. The great emphasis was primarily on experience, and the experimental knowledge of God and His love and His ways. Each member gave an account of God's dealings with him or her, and reported on any remarkable experience, and also their sins and lapses, and so doing compared notes with one another in these respects. The societies were not 'bible study' groups or meetings for the discussion of theology. Of course great stress was laid on reading the Bible as well as prayer, but the more intellectual aspects of the Faith were dealt with in the preaching services and not in the societies. Here, the emphasis was on daily life and living, the fight against the world, the flesh and the devil, and the problems that arise inevitably in the Christian's pilgrimage through this world of sin.

At first the preachers themselves were able to conduct these societies, but as the numbers soon greatly multiplied it became necessary to appoint lay leaders to conduct the various local societies. The preachers now became superintendents of a number of local societies which they visited periodically for the purpose of examination and giving advice.

Of these preachers and leaders the Rev. William Williams, the great hymn-writer and poet, though second to Howell Harris in organising ability, soon became the outstanding and recognised leader and authority in this respect.

The task of conducting these 'experience meetings' obviously called for great wisdom, spiritual insight, tact, and discretion. They could easily degenerate into exhibitionism on the part of extroverts, and lead to scandal, as very private matters were related involving others. It was in order to obviate such troubles and disasters, and to instruct the leaders in this most important work, that the Rev. William Williams wrote this little book now translated into English for the first time.

His genius, his spiritual understanding, and what would now be described as psychological insight stand out everywhere and are truly astonishing.

The experimental or experiential aspect of the Christian life has been seriously neglected during the present century. Certain factors and tendencies have led to this unfortunate condition. Chief among these has been a superficial evangelism which has neglected real conviction of sin and repentance and encouraged an easy believism. Secondly, there has been a theory of sanctification, more psychological than spiritual and scriptural, which has discouraged self-examination and taught that we have only to 'leave it to the Lord'. Thirdly, and more recently, has been an unbalanced emphasis on intellectual understanding of Truth, the social application of Truth, and the manifestation of particular spiritual gifts.

All this has greatly impoverished the spiritual life of both the individual Christian and the churches, and led to coldness, barrenness, and loss of power. The greatest need of the hour is a return to the emphases of the Evangelical Awakening. It is in the belief that this classic of the spiritual life and warfare can greatly stimulate and hasten that return that I encouraged my wife to translate it, and am now happy to commend it, and to advise all Christians to read it. I would particularly urge ministers and pastors to read it, not only because it will prove to be an invaluable help in what is now called counselling of individuals, but also because I would press upon them the importance of introducing such meetings into the life of their churches. Much untold blessing would follow.

D. M. LLOYD-JONES.

I

An imaginary history of the deadness of the land of sleep—the descent of the Spirit on a number of lukewarm professing Christians—the wonderful effect of this—tribulations follow—the means that were used to save the believers from being seduced—the value of the experience meeting in this respect.

THEOPHILUS: Welcome home, Eusebius; it seems an age since I saw you last. I've been longing to meet you in some place or other; but good comes from patient waiting—here's an end to my wishing.

EUSEBIUS: I wanted to see you just as much, if not more, my old companion. My coming to you now is proof enough of that, for my whole object is simply to be able to talk with you about religious matters.

THEOPHILUS: A good purpose, my brother. Do good, and the Lord will prosper it. It would be hard to find a more profitable way of spending time, than in talking gravely and seriously about matters of eternal weight, as we read in Malachi 3: 16, 'Then they that feared the Lord spake often one to another: and the Lord hearkened, and heard it, and a book of remembrance was written before him for them that feared the Lord, and that thought upon his name.'

But first, let me ask how things are with you—are you in good health? What conditions are you living in? Are you happy? Are you married or widowed, rich or poor, respected or despised?

EUSEBIUS: I am perfectly happy in all conditions, so long as I may be near to God in my spirit, for I have learned in whatsoever state I am, therewith to be content; I know both how to be abased and I know how to abound; and I make every effort to be in that condition approved by the Apostle in 1 Corinthians 7: 29, etc.—'that both they that have wives be as though they had none; and they that weep, as though they wept not; and they that rejoice, as though they rejoiced not; and they that buy, as though they possessed not; and they that use this world, as not abusing it.' I thank my God that there is no affliction, cross or sorrow laid upon me, but that my heavenly Father gives me the power to bear it and to be willing.

THEOPHILUS: And now, what progress is the Lord's work making in your country? I have heard that the gospel of Jesus has reached you, and has begotten many sons. Will you please tell me how grace began to work there? By what means? And with what power? And to what extent apart from the usual means? And which graces appeared first? What wiles has Satan devised to hinder the work? And what troubles or trials have you suffered to test and strengthen you and to purify you?

EUSEBIUS: You have asked me many questions, and I will do my best to answer them all, for I find nothing sweeter to recount, and nothing to quicken my soul more, than to remember the days of the Lord's visitation to me and to others in the day of my betrothal to Him, the joyful day of my heart; to remember that time, to me, is ever as sweet as honey.

This is the way the Lord worked in that part of the world. One time, there were just a few of us, professing believers, gathered together, cold and unbelievably dead, in a meeting which we called a special service, so discouraged as to doubt whether we should ever meet again, some who were usually absent from every meeting, some in a deadly apathy, with nothing to say of God nor of their own souls, some given over to the world and its cares, some backslidden completely from all the means of grace and the ordinances of the gospel, some given over to the flesh and its lusts, as in the days of Noah—seeking a wife, seeking a husband, marrying and giving in marriage—and I myself well nigh disheartened and thinking often of coming to live in warmer spiritual climes, and moving my tent from Ur of the Chaldees nearer to the borders of the Promised Land. But, even though all things were as I have described them—the world, the flesh and Satan victorious—these special services were yet conducted in an incredibly lifeless manner. There was no encouragement for anyone to carry on the work, save only the promise of God, that wherever there were if only two or three coming together in His name, if their purpose were right, however lifeless their present state, He would come to them and bless them. This alone had made us come together to pray; but our prayers were not much more than groans.

But at last, forced by cowardice, unbelief and the onslaughts of Satan, we resolved to give up our special meeting; and now we were about to offer a final prayer, fully intending never again to meet thus in fellowship. But it is when man reaches the lowest depths of unbelief that God imparts faith, and when man has failed, then God reveals Himself. So here, with us in such dire straits, on the brink of despair, with the door shut on every hope of success, God Himself entered into our midst, and the light of day from on high dawned upon us; for one of the brethren—yes, the most timid of us all, the one who was strongest in his belief that God would never visit us—while in prayer, was stirred in his spirit and laid hold powerfully on heaven, as one who would never let go. His tongue spoke unusual words, his voice was raised, his spirit was aflame, he pleaded, he cried to God, he struggled, he wrestled in earnest, like Jacob, in the agony of his soul. The fire took hold of others—all were awakened, the coldest to the most heedless took hold and were warmed; the spirit of struggling and wrestling fell on all, we all went with him into the battle, with him we laid hold upon God, His attributes, His Word and His promises, resolving that we would never let go our hold until all our desire should be satisfied.

And this came to pass, for there fell upon us the sweet breath of the love of the Lord. We were filled as if with the fulness of the bowls and the horns of the altar—the fire was kindled and we gave voice with our tongues. The cloud melted away, the sun shone, we drank of the fruit of the vines of the promised land, and we were made to rejoice. Gone was unbelief—gone guilt—gone fear—gone a timid, cowardly spirit, lack of love, envy, suspicion, together with all the poisonous worms that tormented us before; and in their place came love, faith, hope, a joyful spirit, with a glorious multitude of the graces of the Holy Spirit. Up till now the service was only beginning, for prayer, singing, praise and blessing were redoubled, and no one felt like bringing things to an end; and now some were weeping, some praising, some singing, some filled with heavenly laughter, and all full of wonder and love and amazement at the Lord's work—to my mind like the time of the Apostles, when the Spirit descended from on high on a handful of fearful people, and strengthened them mightily to come out of their secret hiding place into the midst of the streets of Jerusalem, and to declare the Name of the Lord before every tribe, tongue and nation that had gathered together there, from the uttermost parts of the earth. As it was then, so it was here now.

This sound went forth and was spread from parish to parish and from village to village, until innumerable people were carrying around the burning word—men and youths, women and children. Preachers, too, came to us from all parts, having heard at a distance rumours of these workings of God; and neither did they come with dry breasts, for, whatever they were to others, they were full of milk for us, because hardly one of them came to us without a true commission—each one's certificate on his lips, for the Lord prospered them in every degree—the sermons were a delight, the listeners plentiful, thoughtful, and eager to listen. There were some convicted in every service—a lad, seeing the change in his friend, drinking in conviction—one sister from another—husband from wife, wife from husband, and lovers bringing one another under conviction. Now the tone of the whole district was changed; instead of playing games on the Sabbath, dancing, cursing, swearing, blaspheming the name of God, singing unworthy songs, empty talk, gossiping, collecting stories, lying and persecuting God's people—instead of all this, I say, the shepherds would sing hymns in the valleys, the ploughman and the driver of his oxen often singing psalms and spiritual songs together in the fields; the maidens, the children and the old men together discoursing happily about the works of the Spirit of grace.

During those days I thought many times of the prophecies of the Old Testament, and I never saw them opened out and explained better than by the heavenly authority on our little church at that time, and on the neighbouring districts; like that Scripture in Joel 2: 29, 30, etc.—'And it shall come to pass afterward, that I will pour out my Spirit upon all flesh; and your sons and your daughters shall prophesy, your old men shall dream dreams, your young men shall see visions. And also upon the servants and upon the handmaids in those days will I pour out my Spirit. And I will show wonders in the heavens and in the earth, blood, and fire, and pillars of smoke.' For to the flesh and the natural man this wonderful work of heaven was as aweful and as fearful as blood and vapour, smoke and fire, to timid men.

THEOPHILUS: Does this same heavenly authority continue still?

EUSEBIUS: The Spirit of the Lord abides with us, and I believe He always will. It is true that those sweet breezes do not blow as frequently as they did, and there is not the same heat in the fire; and the gusts of emotion are less fiery, possibly because there is less of the flesh mixed with them; for, at first, when our souls began to taste the heavenly feasts, the flesh would insist on having its share, and all the natural passions—disturbed by grace—would create a great commotion and noise outside the walls; but as the heavenly feast became more and more enjoyed inwardly in the soul, the flesh has a much lesser part to play than it did, for it has to be silent before the Lord, and leave the soul free to enjoy and to feed itself on the life everlasting. But yet there are obvious signs that these people are going on from grace to grace, for it can be seen that their hearts are wounded and bruised, their consciences alive and tender, their wills broken to the will of God, ready to say with the Apostle: 'What wouldst Thou have me to do?' Godly fear grows in them, and they are careful in all their duties to God, to themselves and to their neighbours—making every effort to keep their place in a seemly way. But their growth is more particularly in the following things.

First, their view of themselves, that their hearts are deceitful above all things, that they are an unruly evil—who can know them? And that —as God Himself says—'Every imagination of the thoughts of his (man's) heart was only evil continually' (Genesis 6: 5). This view makes them loathe themselves, and to believe always that they are the chief of sinners; this causes them not to condemn nor be prejudiced against other people, but to have compassion on all, believing themselves to be more unworthy than anyone.

In the second place, their growing awareness of their need of a Mediator. This poor view of themselves mentioned above has made Christ, and all that pertains to Him, very precious—His righteousness, His sufferings, His power and His wisdom. These people, today, want to look to, to think of, to study nothing but the mercy, the bounty and the gentleness of the Messiah; the suffering on Calvary's hill is what they sing about. This is the subject of their talk and of their study; and they never look inwards (into themselves) except in order to compel themselves to lean more on Christ and to believe more on Him. Thus the bad that they found taught them to run to the good; their sin taught them to look to a Mediator. Thus they were made, to a greater degree, dead to their own gifts, graces, virtues and the good opinions of other people. Today, nothing counts but Christ, and He is all in all.

THEOPHILUS: A hundred to one against Satan leaving such a flock of sheep in peace without causing some havoc among them—at least tempting them, troubling them and oppressing them, or drawing them into some false pleasure.

EUSEBIUS: Oh, I can never tell you everything about these things, because their temptations are innumerable, and of every kind; some for all ranks, some for all ages, some within, some without, some both within and without at the same time, so that no one knows their force or their number save God Himself. But you will understand some of them when you consider their (the flock's) ages and circumstances—companies of merry, manly youths, crowds of girls in the full strength of their feminine attractiveness and vivacity, men who for the most part are an easy prey for Satan to work upon their fleshly lusts, and to entice them to the pleasures of flesh and blood. It is the greatest wonder that they are standing firmly in the midst of all their diverse temptations; it is as great a wonder as it would be for a spark from a fire not to be quenched in the midst of the seas, or for the friends of David to go through the midst of the host of the Philistines to fetch him water from the well of Bethlehem, and yet their lives to be spared. But to heaven are all the thanks due—the One who taught David's fingers to fight, the One who strengthened him to stride through the army and to leap over the wall, strengthened them, too, in spite of their weakness, to defeat Satan on his own ground.

It is true that some of them were wounded, but none was killed; some were sorely tempted, and were lured away to a far country, and thrown down on to cruel rocks; yet their wounds were healed, their bruises and hurts were anointed, and today they are as strong as they ever have been, and much more afraid of going astray than those who have not been tempted. Through being convicted and corrected by the brethren, and through their earnest pleadings and prayers, and by all means of gentle dealing with them, they were pulled out like brands from the burning, and today their song of thankfulness ascends to heaven above.

THEOPHILUS: Of all the means of grace, I know of none more profitable than the special fellowship meetings, called private societies, to correct, to direct, to edify and to encourage weak members who are ever ready to stray aside—either to lusts, pleasures or the love of vanities on the one hand, or to pride, arrogance, conceit and envy on the other; or to be carried about by sleight of men and cunning craftiness to false and erroneous doctrines, and to various other things that have done great harm to the saints of God.

EUSEBIUS: That is my chief business with you, my dear brother and former teacher—to receive some guidance from you (as I have done many times in the past) about these secret services. I believe that they are truly necessary, and that they are, if properly conducted, one of the most authoritative means of keeping the Church of God on the right lines. But some of our people say that there is no basis for them in Holy Scripture, and that that kind of secret gathering was not a custom in the Jewish church, nor in the New Testament either, nor with the Protestant Reformers, but that it is some new order introduced by the Methodists, and that it is profitable for nothing but to teach men to be worse than before, by revealing to each other the secret works of the devil. Some say that it is not a good thing to reveal the secrets of the heart, as there are bad results from doing this. Others maintain that relating experiences leads to pride, and that it is not profitable for all to hear the various temptations that others meet with. And if all were to tell everything, people might become cold towards each other, marriages be broken, lovers fall out on the brink of matrimony, and various scabs and corruptions come to light that no one knew about save God alone.

For this reason, dear Theophilus, show me, so that I may be able to show, to those who doubt the sure foundation of such a religious fellowship as this, their true basis, together with an indication of how far one should go in declaring his mind and heart in such a fellowship. What should be said? What should be avoided? What should be said to God, that is better not said to man? These things, and many more like them, I want, if the Lord wills, to know from you before I leave you.

II

The benefits of the experience meeting when properly used, a proof that it is necessary—its beginnings seen in the Old Testament and the New—the case for being careful lest offences should arise in it—the heavenly wisdom that should be exercised in order that all should be done to edification.

THEOPHILUS: If there were not one instance or example to be found in the Old Testament or the New, the benefit to be derived from such meetings is in itself enough to confirm the fact that they are according to the will of God. There are many things that the Scriptures do not set out as duties; yet, from the very reasonableness of the thing, it is clear enough that they are necessary—such things as family prayers morning and evening, the monthly sacrament, with women allowed to partake of it, prayer before and after the sermon, and many similar things that one can find no clear instance of in the Scriptures, but which can only be deduced from results; yet, such reasonable, profitable and edifying things that hardly anyone would doubt their rightness, except the Quakers.

EUSEBIUS: But I shall be asked how it can be demonstrated that they are so necessary and profitable.

THEOPHILUS: First of all they are so, because they are means of keeping up this same warmth and liveliness that was ours at the beginning; as iron sharpeneth iron, so a man sharpeneth the countenance of his friend. Fellowship is very effective in stimulating us to good or evil; and what better means of maintaining liveliness than to gather together to pray together, to sing together and to declare the goodness of God to one and another since the last meeting; relating the deliverances of the Lord, revealing the way in which God has freed us from the snare of the fowler, and how He has saved us from the noisome pestilence? God's people come away from such a meeting as this like drunkards from the wine-shop—contentedly happy, having drunk the wine of heaven; all comforted, guided and edified. Some possibly, chastened in love, leaving the meeting fully resolved to have done with their lusts; others, weighed down before by trials, discouragement and unbelief, now strengthened in the faith.

In the second place, this kind of fellowship is profitable to unravel the various nets and hidden snares woven by Satan to catch the simple believer on his own ground. The devil is a cunning and crafty spirit, and uses all his ingenuity to bring about the fall of the believer; and like every fisherman he colours his nets, so that the believer cannot see them. He may transform himself into an angel of light, often making his temptations appear as though they were lovely graces, which would, but for the keeping power of God, be able completely to deceive the very elect; and because of this it is a good thing for the saints to come together to search out, and to enquire, and to seek to recognise the temptations that have snared the weak, and to resort to earnest prayer to free their feet from the fetters. Many young saints are like lambs, that run after the dogs instead of after their mothers; imagining that some sins are no sins, but grace; that the breezes of nature are the breath of heaven; that the spirit of melancholy is a truly broken heart; and pride, envy, and prejudice are a sign of zeal for God; and it is necessary for the godly to gather together to extricate weak Christians from these snares, and to direct those who have lost the right way back into it again.

Thirdly, these special fellowship meetings are good at forestalling contentions, suspicions, prejudices, discords, jealousies and all uncharitableness. For people to keep away from each other in the same church (when there is every opportunity for meeting frequently) engenders a lack of love and extreme coldness; and Satan never seeks a better means of kindling these things just mentioned than to get us to neglect this fellowship with one another. The gardener has only to neglect to visit his garden, and to refrain from weeding it, and it will be overrun with weeds in a few weeks; and the church of God need only keep at a distance the one from the other, and lack of love will grow like a root, and from it will come every sorry, miserable branch, and none can destroy it save God alone. But on the other hand, what love, what concord, what good intentions, what security and what protection there is for the members of a church who do not neglect the gathering of themselves together!

In the fourth place we may say that such a gathering together is profitable in order that we may look after and watch over each other's lives, lest any should fall into loose living and turn the grace of God into lasciviousness. The saints of the Most High God often happen to have their abodes in stony places; some with their duties among a host of ungodly men; wealthy farmers, shopkeepers, merchants, or manservants and maidservants to such as these, where they must talk to, mix with, and work with unbelievers, and where they are in great danger of having their garments stained by their proximity to them—either by being lured to pleasures, or by being driven to unseemly outbursts of passion—bitter words, pert answers, or some behaviour unseemly for a believer; and because of this, it is necessary for the people of God to come together to teach each other how to stand in such circumstances, and to correct each other if any have strayed from the right path through the enticements or the oppositions of these unbelievers. As is the custom with girls, when they are dressing and adorning themselves, to look at each other's clothes in case there should be any untidy or unsuitable thing, or something not in keeping with the other garments, so the Church of God, she who has descended from heaven like a bride adorned for her husband, is to look each member at the life and behaviour of the others, for fear that anyone might have formed a bosom friendship with an ungodly world—drinking in the worldlings' customs, speaking their language, giving them their love and their confidences—and in doing so have strayed from the heavenly paths. And what better way is there of doing this than by keeping these special fellowship meetings?

In the fifth place, these fellowship meetings give us the opportunity of bearing one another's burdens. How many of the godly are bearing heavy burdens! Some children have laid burdens on the shoulders of their parents; some parents have done the same to their children; the persecutors and oppressors of this world have laid burdens on many widows and orphan children; some godly men have laid burdens on each other's shoulders—so that a great multitude of believers are groaning beneath the weight of pressures innumerable. And what better way is there of lightening the burden on the shoulders of believers than to let them relate the account of their crosses, their troubles and their tribulations to the people of God? For through this they will not merely get sympathy, but in addition they will have brethren to pray for them, to comfort them and to be kind to them, and to instruct them how to behave under burdens and tribulations; and it gives great relief to every burdened man, when another comes under the yoke with him and takes on himself some of the burden.

In the sixth place, this kind of meeting is profitable because it gives us the opportunity to declare the work of God on our souls, and to praise His name for it. David calls upon the saints (Psalm 66: 16) saying: 'Come and hear, all ye that fear God, and I will declare what he hath done for my soul'. And every one, who is of the same spirit as David, again longs to declare the great things that God has done to him, wanting all the Lord's people to give thanks on his behalf. Oh! how difficult it is for a man who has received great treasures, and those all unexpectedly, either from a loved one or in any other way, not to reveal this to all those who would rejoice with him! The woman who found the silver piece that she had lost could not conceal the matter, but called her friends together, saying: 'Rejoice with me; for I have found the piece which I had lost'. How much greater the desire of a godly man, who has been long in darkness and has now come into the light, to tell of the Lord's mercies to him! Oh! the joy of contemplating the forgiveness of sins! Of viewing the eternal love of the Lord and of the treasures of grace in the promises of the New Covenant!—it is such that a believer cannot refrain from telling it forth with the greatest joy.

But, lastly, these fellowship meetings are profitable for strengthening ourselves against all our spiritual enemies, and for praying together as one man against them all. When Satan finds us one by one on our own, he is more likely to intimidate us; but when the men of God's army come together like this to talk about the powers of heaven, and to tell how the keys of the bottomless pit are in the possession of the Messiah, bringing to mind the works of the Lord in times past—in the Red Sea and the plains of Soar, how He turned the river back, and we went through it on foot—as they recount thus the wonderful works of God, they gain new strength against their spiritual enemies, the world, the flesh and the devil, and part from each other confidently, cheerfully and courageously, as those who had won the day.

These things, and many other things like them, show how profitable are the special meetings of this kind; and even if none of these spiritual matters were to bring godly men together, yet there are various temporal matters and church matters that give them a clear call to foregather; at the moment I may only mention one of these, and that is, to look into the needs of the poor and needy in the churches. While godly men are strangers to each other, there is no doubt that they fall short in this matter; but if the special fellowship meetings are kept in the right way, each one will know the circumstances of the others; and so, compassion, sympathy, generosity, love, brotherly kindness, and every other grace which is meet to be shown by the rich to the poor, the healthy to the sick, by the one who has all to the one who has nothing, by those who are at ease to the miserable and needy, will be exercised.

Here, my dear Eusebius, are things which make the keeping of the private society a clear duty for the people of God—to keep it with the utmost diligence, devotion and application. But with regard to getting a foundation for it from the Word of God, as you have mentioned, there is no difficulty about that either.

SCRIPTURE PROOFS

In the book of Job, which some suppose to be the earliest part of the Scriptures to be written, and that Moses was the author, we find the sons of God[1] (for in those days the godly were called the sons of God, and the ungodly the sons of men) coming to present themselves before the Lord, and Satan also coming among them; their gathering, without a doubt, was a select one, drawn from those who had taken the name of the Lord upon them, and not a mixed multitude of those coming together to hear the word as in New Testament times. For this reason we can call this gathering—into which Satan had entered, our Lord being present too—a select gathering or a private society, for we are not told that anyone here was giving any special address with a multitude of the sons of men listening; no one but the sons of God, that is, the followers of the true God.

Again, in Genesis 4:26 we find Enos, grandson of Adam, gathering together the few who were faithful to the worship of the living God in his day; and there, as one fellowship, they began to call upon the name of the Lord. This was between 250 and 300 years after the creation of the world; and God seemed to have been forgotten, and idol worship had entered among the descendants of Cain, and there was none but Enos in the family of Adam sufficiently alive spiritually to gather the people together in a religious fellowship. In the days of Abraham the church in his house numbered a thousand, or many more, followers of the true God, and, doubtless, a man such as Abraham would have discipline, a good ordering of matters, and a performance of all religious duties among them, and he himself as the head of the family acting as their priest; and whatever may be profitable, edifying and proper to be in a private society, Abraham doubtless fulfilled all, according to the understanding of those dark days.

It says in Malachi 3, at a time when the Jewish church had backslidden a long way from her first pure estate: 'Then they that feared the Lord spake often one to another: and the Lord hearkened, and heard it, and a book of remembrance was written before him for them that feared the Lord, and that thought upon his name. And they shall be mine, saith the Lord of hosts, in that day when I make up my jewels (or in the day when I gather my peculiar treasure); and I will spare them, as a man spareth his own son that serveth him.' There you have the full story of special fellowship meetings and how they appear in God's sight. You have often heard from the lips of the enemies of the Christian faith about the book of life found in the private societies—how that the names of all the members are kept in it, and that a certain person writes the name, forgives the sin, and receives payment for the service rendered. All this is but one more of the tens of thousands of lies spread by the

[1] William Williams's interpretation here would no longer be accepted.

people of this world; but the verses quoted above reveal the secret that God is keeping a book of remembrance of these religious societies, and listens to their prayers, keeps them and defends them, as a man spares his son that serves him. You see that God is the Head of the society, it is He that keeps the book, it is He Himself that writes the names, it is He that proclaims forgiveness, and it is He that gathers together the people of the societies, in the day of judgment, as a peculiar treasure for Himself.

The prophet Zechariah in the twelfth chapter, writing prophetically about the days of the gospel, says that God will pour upon the house of David, and upon the inhabitants of Jerusalem, the spirit of grace and of supplications; and the effect of that spirit will be that they shall look upon the Messiah, whom they have pierced, and shall mourn for Him as one mourneth for his only son, and shall be in bitterness for Him, as one that is in bitterness for his firstborn. And their mourning shall be great, even as the mourning of Hadad-rimmon in the valley of Megiddon. And in this, their mourning, every family shall remain apart—the family of the house of David apart, and their wives apart; the family of the house of Levi apart, and their wives apart; the family of Shimei apart, and their wives apart; all the families that remain, every family apart, and their wives apart. You see here, in the first place, that this is a prophecy of the days of the gospel, for the sole cause of this mourning is that they pierced Christ with their sins. Secondly, that an evangelical mourning, for having sinned against a Mediator so gentle, so glorious and so faithful, is beyond every other mourning under the sun, yes, even mourning for an only-begotten son. In the third place, that those people gathered themselves together to grieve together and to mourn together. Fourthly, that they did not all gather together in any one place, as in time past to the temple, but in small fellowships, the house of David, the house of Levi, the house of Simeon, and the other families by themselves. In the fifth place, we have here the family divided in two, the men in one fellowship, the women in the other; and if any one text of Scripture is enough to persuade men, this is enough to show them that to have a society of men by themselves, and a society of women by themselves, is not only lawful, but also that it had been prophesied of them in the Old Testament that this was to be the case in the New, when there would be an outpouring of the Spirit of the Lord upon the Church of God. And, according to these Scriptures, the 'society bands' are but the result of the outpouring of the Holy Spirit; and this arrangement is a necessity too, because this society is one for the confessing of weaknesses and corruptions that pierce the Messiah, and because of this it is not a good thing for men to know the lapses of the women, nor, on the other hand, for the women to hear of the weaknesses of the men, lest Satan—ready at all times to take advantage—should make use of these things to multiply sin and temptation for the one and the other.

In the New Testament, we find our Lord and His Apostles, at various times, separating themselves from the common people and withdrawing to the mountain, or the sea, and, last of all, to the garden of Gethsemane; and whenever this happened, He would be sure to open out the parables for them, and reveal various great truths about the Kingdom of heaven—things that at the time they did not understand, but after the outpouring of the Spirit they remembered them and understood them too.

After the crucifixion of our Lord, after He had appeared to Mary Magdalene, to Peter, and to two other disciples on the road to Emmaus, the Apostles, and others of His disciples, together with Mary, the mother of Jesus, and some of the other women, gathered themselves together at Jerusalem to hold a special fellowship meeting to await the unfolding of the object and the purpose of all the things that had recently happened in Jerusalem; and while they were there recounting—some how they had seen Him in one place, and especially how the two disciples had recognised Him in the breaking of the bread, and how their hearts were burning in the way as He opened unto them the Scriptures—while they were speaking of these things, Jesus Himself came and stood in their midst, and said to them, 'Peace be unto you'. Here was a 'private society' pleasing to God, a society of which Jesus became a member; and what was there for them to do before He came, but to speak together of the loss to them without Him, how bereft they all were, and of the comfortable hope enjoyed by most of them that He was risen from the dead, and that He would stay with them on earth? This ever shows clearly that the best procedure for believers in all conditions, and especially in times of misery, fear and perplexing providences, is to maintain regular attendance at the religious fellowships, until the day dawn, and the Lord Himself come into the midst.

After the ascension of our blessed Lord into heaven, when His disciples were in great fear of the Jews, and were gathered together into one place in Jerusalem, and there continuing in prayer and pleading till the feast of Pentecost was come, 'suddenly there came a sound from heaven as of a rushing mighty wind, and it filled all the house where they were sitting. And there appeared unto them cloven tongues like as of fire, and it sat upon each of them. And they were all filled with the Holy Ghost, and began to speak with other tongues, as the Spirit gave them utterance.' Here was an outstanding meeting, with the blessing of heaven upon it; and the religious fellowships which truly wait upon the Lord share the same effects, but to a lesser degree, as the disciples here, for our Lord has said that whenever two or three are gathered together in His name, He will be there in the midst to bless them; and when do people gather together in His name more surely than in the private society, when the only business of the majority, if not indeed of all, is to meet with the Lord?

Paul enjoins the believers in Hebrews 10: 'Not forsaking the assembling of ourselves together, as the manner of some is; but exhorting one another: and so much the more, as ye see the day approaching.' And see the awful effects of neglecting the gathering of ourselves together, in verse 26—'For if we sin wilfully'—that is, if we depart from seeking after God, the Christian sacraments, the means of grace, and the fellowship and friendship of the saints—'after that we have received the knowledge of the truth, there remaineth no more sacrifice for sins, but a certain fearful looking for of judgment and fiery indignation, which shall devour the adversaries.' Oh! how awful it is to begin to backslide from God! And very often the first beginning of backsliding shows itself in a coldness towards the company and peculiar fellowship of the saints. And in the third chapter of Hebrews we are bidden to 'exhort one another daily, while it is called To day; lest any of you be hardened through the deceitfulness of sin'—which shows that the Holy Spirit means us, first, to gather ourselves together, and then to exhort each other lest we depart from the living God.

* * *

EUSEBIUS: This satisfies me for the time being as to the scriptural authority for these special meetings, but alas! O God, that I and others might know how to conduct them in such a way that they may be blessed! For though the thing is good in and of itself, yet if the sacraments of God, and all the means of grace, and the duties of the gospel, are not carried out according to the pattern shown on the mount, with honest purpose, and in the Spirit of the Lord, letting His pillar of fire and pillar of the cloud go before, the grace of God could be turned to lasciviousness; and so, by misuse, the best thing be turned into the worst thing. This is how the Church of Rome turned the sacrament of the Lord's Supper into a superstitious spell to blind the mind and to steal the money of the ignorant common people. I have heard that some churches have received no small damage from some young people in their first enthusiasm. These young people, looking neither before nor behind, but with the utmost zeal for God and the utmost hatred of sin, dwelt and dilated so much on their corruptions, though God had forgiven them, that it did themselves much harm afterwards and was also harmful to the good name of some of their neighbours.

Again, without a doubt, some people known to me myself have deeply offended weak believers by rebuking them harshly, correcting them sharply, and speaking boorishly to people of their sins, even to those who had not received grace, nor had a natural temperament that would suffer such rebukes, devoid of all love, sympathy and compassion; and through this they became hardened yet more in their faults and were driven out of that church into another. But the worst fault in our special society is the reciting of weaknesses, downfalls and hurts that some of us have experienced, in an unbroken, sound and healthy spirit, with no sorrow for sin, so that the recital of these things has the same effect on others as it does on the spirit of the one reciting them. This makes the wound worse instead of healing it, and spreads the plague instead of stopping it; for to hear of the weaknesses and downfalls of others in an unbroken spirit inflames the passions further and nurtures lust; and if and when an opportunity comes to the careless man that heard of his brother's fall, a hundred to one that he, too, will fall, not against his will, but wilfully, into the same pit. And so, through faulty methods, lightness of spirit and lack of wisdom, this lovely fellowship, that once was a sweet smelling savour to God, and would still be had it kept on the right lines, is now, from misuse, an unsavoury offence to His holiness.

THEOPHILUS: Wisdom alone is to direct, to edify and to enlighten in these religious fellowships, and it is quite presumptuous to lay down many rules, disciplines and orders for the sake of keeping them and sticking to them, without, above all, waiting on the Spirit of the Lord to trouble the water. On the other hand, it is true that rules, as a means in the hand of the Holy Spirit, are profitable, are blessed, and are used in every society as a ladder to climb to bring us to God.

III

The absolute necessity for stewards in an experience meeting—their gifts, and the burden that should be upon their spirits for the work of God—instructions concerning teachers, some of whom may be in doubt as to whether they have been called to preach the Gospel of Christ or not.

EUSEBIUS: Tell me a little about these rules, and I believe that my heavenly Father will make them a blessing to me and to my society.

THEOPHILUS: Well, then—it is essential that there should be stewards in every fellowship. There is no family without a head, and no church without a minister, nor any parish without its warden; and how unsuitable to have a society without a head or a steward! Let the number of stewards be according to the number of the people: where a fellowship consists of many scores of members, it is necessary to have more; and if the members live at distances from each other, it is necessary that one steward, if possible, should come from each district, so that he might be familiar with the daily life and conduct of each member that lives in that district; but if the society consists of only a few, arrangements convenient to the circumstances must be made.

EUSEBIUS: What would be the functions of these stewards? It seems to me that they would be head over everybody—old and young, poor and rich in their society; therefore I presume that they ought to be very highly gifted—their experience, their wisdom, their discretion and their cautiousness excelling all others in the society; and above all they need to have a clear-eyed ability to recognize the temperament, the emotions, the troubles and the inclinations of all the different ages and ranks of the members of the fellowship. It seems to me that they would be expected to have the spirit of a father, a brother, a mother and a nurse—to be harsh with some, and to pull them like brands from the burning; and to be more gentle with others—to comfort the weak-minded, to strengthen the feeble and to bind up the broken-hearted, but to rebuke sharply those who have sinned and show no signs of repentance—those who break the commandments of God, and teach others to break them. But, my honoured teacher, I will leave you to show what the office of these stewards should be, and what gifts are fitting for them to possess, for my purpose in coming here was to be taught by you.

THEOPHILUS: As to their gifts, the greater they are, the better; but to have spiritual graces in their hearts excels over gifts, for if they had the gifts of all the Apostles and the Prophets, yet if true godliness has not possessed their spirit, they are nothing but 'sounding brass' or 'a tinkling cymbal'; and they cannot be whole-hearted in desiring to further the work of God if they themselves have never known the God for whom they are working. And no one can ever be honest, gentle, clear and lively, to convince and convict, to rebuke, to edify and to comfort the people of God, unless he himself belongs to God.

But as to their gifts, as you have said, it is a very good thing if they have the gifts you mention. Many a religious society, however, is so weak and timid, so ignorant and feeble that there is not one member among them with the qualifications which you have mentioned. For that reason, one must take them as they are, or be without; and yet, though they may not have the enlightenment, the experience and the wisdom already mentioned, it is necessary that they have the following gifts, and if they are devoid of these it is not right to elect them as stewards, for these are things which belong to their office in the church.

In the *first* place they must have a bold spirit, free from the fear of man; for if they are governed by the fear of man, not only are they under the curse of the Scriptures, but moreover they cannot do their work honestly, for a slavish fear will hold them back from any good that they might do, and they will speak the truth only to those of low degree, and possibly not even to them.

Secondly, it is necessary that those who hold this office must feel a sincere love to the whole fellowship, regarding all the members as their brethren and sisters in the Lord. Without this heavenly disposition they will sympathize with none, but will be hard, boorish and unpleasant—revealing secret faults before all, making things appear worse than they are, being more forgiving to some than to others, and various other unfortunate results which come into being in any office in the church which is held without a sincere love for all the members. It is also necessary that these stewards should possess zeal, warmth and life to a greater degree than anyone else in the fellowship, and it is from among the warmest and most zealous that the members should for the most part make their choice; for if the steward is cold and dead and timid, how can such a cold person convince, convict and rebuke? How can he comfort and console? And how can a sleepy man lead others on, when he does not advance a step himself? Because of this, it is a good thing, if possible, that such office-holders should be lively in their faith, warm in their spirit, promoting God's work with zeal and heavenly enthusiasm —the kind that will keep the meeting alive from beginning to end.

These things, my brother, are absolutely essential in the stewards of a society; and it would be profitable if they had dozens of other things in addition; but the churches are so weak that one cannot find gifts, attributes or graces as one would wish; and so we must take things as they are. But as to their duties, they are something like this, namely, in the first place, to keep the names of all the members in a register, so that they can be called by name one at a time, should any special need arise. Many times Israel was numbered, for instance, on leaving Egypt, and at other times, and that for special reasons. So here; sometimes this would be expedient for collections; sometimes to call the members for catechism or examination; but always useful at every service, to know who is missing; for it would not be out of place for some one of the stewards to read all the names at the end of the meeting, in order to remember, at the next meeting, to ask those absent ones (but present now) the reason for their absence at the previous meeting.

Thirdly, it is the work of the stewards to collect for the needs of the church. The Apostles appointed seven men full of the Holy Spirit, for the sole purpose of collecting and distributing the collection between the poor and worthy members among the churches. So now, it is the stewards who are to urge the wealthy to be generous, and to examine closely the state of the poor—enquiring into their circumstances, insisting on knowing their needs, and supplying their necessities; but taking great care at the same time that none of the poor be idle, or given to boasting or gossiping from house to house; any such should be sharply reprimanded by the stewards and others of the fellowship, and should be made to work with their hands and to eat their bread in the sweat of their brow. But the fellowship is to care for those who are widows indeed, who live unto the Lord and have their trust in God, and yet are poor in this world—to feed them, to clothe them, and if they are sick to appoint suitable people to tend them and to pay for a doctor to visit them. In this way, all the care of the poor of that fellowship will rest on the shoulders of the stewards.

Fourthly, it will be their duty to see that there are teachers to minister the Word, at least on every Sabbath Day, if there is not a settled ministry in that fellowship. Although the connexion as a whole is responsible for the expense, yet the duty of caring for such ministers rests on the shoulder of these stewards—going themselves, or appointing others, to meet them; and after they have ministered, to accompany them some part of the way on their return, attending to them on their journey as they come and as they go, as the women did with the Saviour of the world in the days of His flesh, which thing He suffered them to do, in order to show us our duty of love to the ministers of the Word; for if they have sown unto us spiritual things, it is no great thing for us to recompense them in temporal things.

EUSEBIUS: At this point I want to ask you a question, which has been weighing heavily on me for some time. You know that in these days there is a good measure of respect for preachers—whatever their allegiance—with no persecution, contempt or disregard for any who take this name upon them; rather a better livelihood and an easier existence than before. I am afraid that this has encouraged many good craftsmen to leave their callings and to launch out enthusiastically into preaching, without a backward glance at their lawful calling, confident that they were meant for bigger things, and not doubting that, if they could achieve a few gifts, the blessing would follow them, together with respect, profit and ease, and that they would soon be able to compete with the best teachers, if indeed not to surpass them. Out they went with great zeal like Francis Drake or Fernando Cortes, with high hopes of possessing a better land than the old crafts of building, or shoemaking or cobbling, and indeed, having started they developed (through boldness of spirit, diligent practice and a desire for the office) some kind of gift but with little knowledge. But with this they became proud and showed signs of an 'unbroken' heart, a dry spirit and a desire for the respect and glory of men rather than a desire to win souls from the grip of Satan to the living God.

Today, preachers of all denominations are more numerous than were the Bibles in the dark days of our grandfathers, so that we can have, if we should so desire, four or five sermons in our meeting-house in the same week. Some of them announce that they will preach in places where they have not been invited, and will preach, if they can get a few to listen, within a mile or two of those whom God honours far more than they themselves. Some of these bring with them a great pretence of having heavenly light, divine authority and religious experience surpassing that of others, and for that reason they pontificate and lord it, trampling underfoot or raising up the church of God, as they wish; but bringing with them at the same time a strong savour of pride, vanity, the flesh, self-importance, lust for glory, unbrokenness of spirit and a kind of glibness—all of which a man living close to God cannot endure. Other of these men have a dry, hard, legalistic spirit savouring strongly of envy, bitterness and discontent—very unprofitable to the hearers. Others again give a false impression of great knowledge of wisdom and order by interpreting words, splitting texts, and splintering the Scriptures into innumerable pieces and scattering them abroad, throwing out to ignorant, unlearned people sackfuls of doctrines, subjects, openings, reasonings, notes, matters and exhortations, so that it seems that their chief aim is to show their hearers how knowledgeable they are in the art of divinity; all being carried out without the Spirit of the Lord.

Again, some striplings, who have hardly read their Bibles once through, have launched out, either from their trades, or from school, knowing little or nothing of the work of the Spirit of grace on their souls, they too wanting the opportunity to preach for the purpose of improving their gifts, multiplying their talents and opening doors to becoming respected and acceptable people, in the hope that one day they will make a good fortune from the preaching of the Word. And some, as wrong in their purpose as any of the others, if not worse, go forth in order to promote their own party, and to increase the size of their congregations, and to extend the bounds of their spheres of influence, putting that interest forward by every possible means; sometimes by saying a little openly here and there as they see that the place and the people will receive it; but much oftener by secretly enticing unstable people to leave their proper teachers and sweet teachings, orthodox and experimental, and to come in to feed on their own sour grapes, which thing, in my estimation, is no less an evil than robbery.

I am afraid to invite any of these to come among us, lest they do more harm than good; and yet the ignorant follow one or another of these people and are most zealous on their behalf. Some young people follow the first kind for what they suppose is their zeal and their authority; and are ready to worship them and to support them; and they fawn upon them like spaniels, esteeming all their conceit and their pride to be heavenly graces, though they condemn these things in others; and that even their light, careless, irreverent and wanton attitude and conduct is praiseworthy and glorious. Others follow the dry, harsh and envious preachers, and have drunk so deeply of their spirit that they look like them, sound like them and have the same unloving spirit. Again, some cleave to the orderly preachers (as they are called), holding that there is never a good preacher who does not draw out doctrines, proving them by reasoning and from Scripture, raising points, drawing out lessons, showing consequences and giving exhortations; and that the best sermon of all is the longest, and the one which has the largest number of divisions.

Some again think that the educated young men who break out are wonderful, regarding it as one of the seven wonders of the world that a youngster should speak from a pulpit; and that he is a worthy object of their love, especially if he is fair to look at, beautiful and of an amiable appearance; even though, at bottom, he is nothing but one who wants some day to be a man of many gifts, accepted and praised by the churches. But there are some, again, who cling to the preachers who are always calling for volunteers to fill up their congregations, as the king recruits men to his thinning armies. These are the people who are tired of their own congregations, either because they are too enthusiastic, or the discipline there is too strict, and they want to go somewhere where they could be much freer and less restricted, and where they would receive more respect and be more acceptable. And it would not take long for a crafty, cunning and enticing preacher to win over to his own opinions those whom indifference, prejudice and instability have made ripe for the picking. But, honoured teacher, I will take your advice on how the stewards of the society should act in these cases.

THEOPHILUS: This is a matter which calls for skilful handling, and a matter that requires the greatest possible discretion and grave consideration; and God alone can teach us how to act aright in it. It is perfectly true that, in all the denominations, many set out to preach, who are much more concerned about honours, personal gain and creature comforts, as you say, than for the glory of God and the good of immortal souls; and their preaching has none of the fragrance of the Bridegroom's robes—none of the holy oil, no note of the voice of the divine Dove. Men do not do well when they praise these preachers, encourage them or reward them; on the contrary they should bid them follow their temporal callings, and not rush forward to the Ark of God without a call; they should bid them eat their own bread which they have earned through the sweat of their brow, and not behave like the wasps, despoiling the true honey-bees of their honey, living idly at the expense of poor men, who half starve themselves in order to support the true ministers of the Word.

The Holy Spirit gives us, through the lips of the Apostles, a sharp warning to beware of teachers who have gone astray in their doctrines, their lives, their aims or their spirit. And it was our Lord Himself who said that by their works or by their fruits they shall be known (Matthew chapter 7), which makes us very wary in choosing a preacher, lest we exalt or praise or magnify any before we have time to test whether their doctrines, their lives, their experiences and their private communion with God answer to the witness of the Word.

But on the other hand, my son, do not be too anxious and ready to judge; take time, and prove all things, but hold fast to that which is good. There have been many youths in past years who have broken away from their calling, in their zeal and first love, to preach with little or no learning, and with no purpose other than to promote God's work and to draw men from darkness to light; and the Lord has blessed and used them to this end too. Through their ministry people in some very dark corners have been enabled to hear the Word and come to attend all the means of grace, and some, I have reason to hope, have been effectively called through them. As to these men, it would be a great loss to the Church of God to be deprived of them; and so long as their doctrines are sound, and they continue humble in spirit, living lives becoming to the gospel of Christ, it is no small sin to despise them, though they have no great learning and are lacking in knowledge both literary and historical. Yet, while they have the substance in them—that is, the Spirit of the Lord—you must esteem them highly in every way that is fitting and right for ministers of the gospel; and though they were lately only carpenters, shoemakers and cobblers, as you say, they are none the worse for that, any more than the Apostles, who were all unlearned men except Paul himself, if they continue in the true spirit and adhere to the doctrine of the Church. I know that some preachers, who formerly lived by just such poor trades, are today truly dividing the Word of life—able to teach, to convict, to rebuke, encourage, and catechize, and sounding forth the gospel of Christ in the same spirit as the holy martyrs of old, or the first Reformers from the popish religion, so that no one need be ashamed of them, and neither priest nor bishop can find fault with them, if they are allowed to speak in their own way—because they do not presume to teach the people anything but Jesus Christ and Him crucified, according to the teaching of the true Faith.

For that reason you must take great care whom you despise and whom you honour. Pay respect to whom respect is due, and rebuke him who deserves to be rebuked. And yet, after having tested them out on many occasions, whomsoever you find lacking in the Spirit of the Lord, unsound in their doctrines, unsavoury in their friendships, licentious in conduct, shallow in their aims, dry, dead and legalistic in their ministry, seeking to win men's allegiance to themselves rather than to the living God; or if any show signs that they have no desire to keep close to God themselves and with no likelihood that they would ever be instrumental in drawing others closer to Him—to such as these you must not bid God speed, do not encourage them, do not seek them out or invite them, and do not support them on their journeys. But it is a great pity that in these lifeless gospel days there is no man under heaven that can stop these men roaming round the country, or that can persuade them to read books on church history or some body of divinity, these men who imagine that what they have is enough to make them like bishops in the Church of God. Because of this they flock, without restraint, in multitudes from district to district, from south to north, not humble enough to belong to any fellowship of higher standing than themselves, for fear of losing one degree of the praise that they expect to get there—all of which springs from conceit and spiritual pride.

Well did the Apostle Paul speak a warning to Timothy, his son in the faith, to be very careful in ordaining ministers of the Word, not to lay hands on a novice in the faith, 'lest being lifted up with pride he fall into the condemnation of the devil' (1 Timothy 3: 6). For there is no doubt but that a proud spirit, self-esteem and a pompous bearing are only too ready to ensnare young men who are given prominence before they are mature enough to receive it. And one of the ugliest things that is now to be found in the multitudes of young men going around preaching, in all the denominations, is spiritual pride. It is very easy for anyone who has a perceptive eye to recognize it in any of its various appearances; and the more unlearned, young and lacking in experience the teacher, the uglier is this thing. Alas! how sad it is to see a weak man—weak in understanding, learning and training, puffing himself up, boasting, pushing himself forward, and trying to appear as something most wonderful, as though there were not his like in the whole world; carpenter, shoemaker, weaver or fuller, yes, a raw stripling that one would hardly trust to shepherd his sheep, will today ride his high horse more boldly and with much less modesty than the old ministers who have borne the burden and heat of the day. This poor specimen (carrying his poisonous fruits around with him) is upset by any disappointment, offended at every slight, displeased at every poor reception and difficult to please in any way—there is hardly food, drink, fire in the grate, or bed that will please him. He will grumble, condemn, criticize and trample people underfoot because he cannot get enough love, generosity and courtesy for himself. He wants to be fetched and carried, to be made much of and cherished—in a word, he wants the preacher to be worshipped rather than the God whom he preaches. Oh! it is a pitiful sight to see a teacher puffing himself up with wind, and swelling with spiritual pride at the thought of his own gifts and knowledge, and the good reception he gets in the church, instead of giving with becoming humility a good example in living and behaviour, as well as in doctrine; and behaving in a meek, pleasant, watchful way and full of godly fear in all his associations; he should be easy to deal with, satisfied with the provision made for him, coming and going without grumbling and groaning or showing any kind of discontent, whatever he may get in the way of disappointment, contempt, slight or poor reception.

And if, on account of ill health, low spirits or a tendency to sudden fainting fits, the wives of any teachers have to accompany them, it is fitting that they too should be self-effacing and meek, giving a good example to other wives in all their conduct and behaviour—walking circumspectly, quietly and timidly as it becomes those professing the gospel of Christ—loving their husbands and obeying them in the Lord, not dressing grandly, vainly, and proudly—not appearing lustful, and greedy about food or delicacies, and not being too eager for gossip over tea or coffee, after the manner of the ungodly women of the world; but rather, while thus away from home, spending their time in looking after their husbands, listening and learning, helping burdened housewives to minister to strangers, rising early, cleaning, and mending their husband's clothes and those of their fellow-travellers too, in order to lessen the work of the hostess and make it less burdensome. It is really hurtful for a preacher's wife to be shallow, proud, wanton-eyed, a gossip, and ribald and slanderous; going from house to house and from one district to another with tittle-tattle, like a Gazette for Satan, laying bare her own emptiness, and disgracing her husband by letting the church see that he suffers such a vain woman to have her own way as she will.

EUSEBIUS: You need say no more; I hope that the Spirit of the Lord will enable me to distinguish between teachers and teachers; and I know that I can never be too cold towards the ones that God has not sent, nor too warm towards His true ministers. But now proceed with the functions of the stewards.

THEOPHILUS: Well then, in the *fifth* place, their duty is to rebuke—with all gentleness, compassion and love—those whom they see walking in a way which is unworthy of the gospel of Christ; if a member is fraternizing too much with the ungodly world, given to foolish talking, wanton behaviour, lying; if he is proud, miserly, slanderous, lewd, lascivious, dictatorial and lacking in balance, or showing any sign that he is walking according to the course of this world;—then the stewards, I say, are to take him aside, by himself, and rebuke him—as I said before, with all gentleness. And if such an one is won over to confess and to forsake his fault, they should not bring his case before the fellowship—the stewards have won him back for God; but if he refuses to confess, and if he will not forsake his fault, then the case must be brought before the entire society.

Lastly, it is a very good thing if the stewards are suitably gifted to lead the singing, to pray, to catechize, to comfort, to edify and to perform all the tasks that appertain to the ministry of grace in a society of separated Christians.

IV

The rules of procedure in the meetings of the societies—who is to catechize the members—gifts necessary in the catechists—things that tend to corrupt the catechists, such as fleshly love, showing respect of persons to the great, and the lure of rewards—mistakes made during the process of catechizing—questions that should be put to those being received into fellowship—the witness that should be borne to their lives—the length of time that they should be on trial—the charge laid upon them, together with the duties.

EUSEBIUS: And now, tell me how things should be ordered, when the society meets together like this. Give me some instruction, for I am anxious to know the best way to keep warmth and life in the worship of the Lord.

THEOPHILUS: First of all, let there be prayers and pleadings to God to lead you in the way which pleases Him, whether in singing praises, or continuing in prayer, catechizing some, comforting the weak-minded, rebuking the heedless and careless, or in whatever else has to be done, that all should be done according to the mind and the will of the Lord. As of old ancient Israel was called upon to follow the pillar of cloud and fire, so His saints today are to follow the voice and the leading of His Spirit, so that if His Spirit does not honour one exercise, our duty is to turn to some other. If catechizing is not seen to be progressing with enlightenment, warmth and life, it is better to spend the time in singing or praying, or in some exercise that will promote conviction, instruction and comfort.

EUSEBIUS: But if we are to catechize, who is suitable for the task, pray? For I have heard some men catechizing without one glimmer of light, or any degree of warmth in their examination, so that they darken the minds, not only of those being questioned, but also of the whole gathering, and possibly spend as much time with one as would be needed to catechize six.

THEOPHILUS: Quite true; to catechize is a special gift not possessed by one in a hundred. It has the following elements:

First, the gift of asking questions pertaining to the state of the one being questioned: some catechizers are so ignorant that they put questions to youth that belong to age, or to the poor that pertain to the rich, to the doubting questions more suitable to the presumptuous, and to a man newly converted those suited to a professing believer of sixty years standing.

Secondly, the gifted catechizer asks his questions with enjoyment and sweetness, such as will kindle zeal and enthusiasm in all, and cause the whole company to praise God for the glorious light.

Thirdly, this catechizer understands the state of the man being questioned from the few answers that fall from his lips; and then he lays open the man's condition before the whole fellowship in a much clearer way than the man himself could do, revealing the earliest beginnings of any tendency to error, and the first signs of the heavenly principle of grace and its accompanying gifts. And so, through the experiences of the man being questioned, the catechizer lights a candle of heavenly brightness for the entire fellowship, and provides for them a dish of sweetmeats, possibly even from a poor and muddled experience.

Fourthly, the good catechizer perceives what particular sin it is that keeps the man away from God; he can seek out those dark dens, where lurk sin and Satan, fleshly lusts and the lust of the world and its idols. In the same way as a fisherman knows where the fish are, and the mole-catcher the runs of the moles, and the fowler where to find the partridge, so does the expert catechizer recognize the cause of every fall, so does he recognize the secret ways of the temptations of the world and of the flesh, and know of all the twists and turns of human nature; the difference between stirrings of grace and the stirrings of nature, between true repentance and fits of melancholy, or the state of unhappiness that overtakes us at times in this world. As Sir Isaac Newton, with a few round and triangular figures, comprehends all the circuits of the stars and planets, so the good catechizer, with the word or two that he gets from the lips of a simple man, comes to an exact understanding of the state of that man's heart, and lays it before the entire fellowship, with the result that he has everybody loving and praising the works of the Lord.

There are various gifts and qualities necessary beside these in a fit and authoritative catechizer; and there are some things which present a very real hindrance to honest, faithful and unprejudiced catechizing.

EUSEBIUS: Name some of the things which do harm, and which corrupt the catechizers and prevent them from dealing sincerely in the Lord's work.

THEOPHILUS: To be overfond of people, and that on purely natural grounds, is a great hindrance in this matter. When men are much in each other's company, and bound by friendships, far from making them speak the truth to each other, it often makes them so apt to hide faults and to forgive them that they are unwilling to see any fault in one who is full of faults; for that reason, it is often not fitting or meet for a friend to catechize his closest friend. And secondly, for a poor man to catechize those in high positions in the world becomes unprofitable, because the poor of this world are too ready to respect the persons of the great, and without a strong sense of the presence of the Lord they cannot speak their mind clearly in God's cause.

But there is still another thing that often affects judgment—and it would be a good thing if this sin were found only among worldlings, and it is a very great pity that it is also found among the professors of religion—namely, reward—that thing which, in the same way that it affects judgment among worldly judges, also hinders judgment among professors of religion. This often happens when the members of a religious fellowship show great respect to those who catechize them, and are generous in bestowing the good things of this world upon them; so that this, by kindling love in their hearts towards them, and good opinions of them, tends to make the catechizers to hide and to excuse their faults, however numerous they may be; in this way their usefulness to the fellowship becomes uselessness, because their eyes are completely blinded by gifts and rewards. And men who may come from some remote district to such a religious fellowship, not knowing any of the members, and never having received any kindness from any of them, will catechize more faithfully, simply, and without respect of persons—until they, again, get to know the members of the fellowship and to receive evidences of love at their hands, when they, in their turn, will fall to the same softness as the others, that is, to let love blind their eyes and warp their judgment.

EUSEBIUS: That is quite true, and I know that strangers, who are not familiar with the members, will arrive at the truth and speak more honestly to them, and with less prejudice, than the ones who are always with them; the strangers, I tell you, will hit upon their darling sins, and reveal their state to the whole church much more surely than those who are always with them. Perhaps the cause of it is what you say, that is, carnal love, too close friendship, respect of persons, or the lure of gifts and rewards; but we have to suffer things as they are. But I hope to see better times, when honesty and simplicity, enlightenment and unprejudiced judgment, together with real integrity in God's work, will win the day.

But now, proceed with the matter of this catechizing—how should it be carried out? Because I know of many mistaken ideas about this—some catechizing in an obscure way, a hard way; some asking totally irrelevant questions, some so entangling and confusing the man being questioned that he has nothing to say, and some doing all the talking, so that the man they are questioning can hardly get a word in. Because of all this, give us some guidance in this matter.

THEOPHILUS: The Spirit of the living God alone can really do this aright, and we should not bind ourselves too closely to any one set of rules; yet, it is not unprofitable to show the type or kind of question that is suitable and likely to be blessed in particular cases. But we must understand that we should not be putting the same questions to everyone —not the same question, for instance, to a beginner in Christ as to an older Christian; not the same one to the doubting as to the one enjoying assurance, to the one suffering onslaughts of trials and temptations as to the one dwelling in the bosom of the Lord. But heaven will give wisdom, so that the catechizer whose soul cries out to heaven will never be allowed to run short of profitable and edifying questions.

EUSEBIUS: In the first place, then, discuss the catechizing of those who are to be received into membership—what questions should be put to these? What is the minimum manifestation of grace that admits a person to the society? Should such be allowed in without a trial period? Or, if they must be put on trial, how long should that trial period last? And what demands should be laid upon those who are admitted? and what special duties do they owe to that particular society more than to another?

THEOPHILUS: You must not expect as much of the light of faith and assurance in those newly received into membership as in those already in, who have long enjoyed the visitations of the Lord (though, the more's the pity to think that many who are received in in the early days of their awakening excel in this matter over many who have been in for a long time, and quite possibly have better experiences, themselves, at that time than they will have after they have been members of the fellowship for a long time). But the questions that should be asked are somewhat along the following lines:

1. Have you had a view of your pitiful state, have you seen yourself as alien from the commonwealth of Israel, without hope, and without God in the world? Have you been made to see for certain that you are bound for eternal misery unless God is pleased to have mercy on you, and to give you, in Christ, the right to His own free grace, and that you deserve damnation, and to suffer the judgment of God and man?

2. Have you had one view of yourself as a greater sinner than anyone else, so that whatever faults you may have seen or heard to be in others, you see your own sin as greater and uglier, and deserving, on many accounts, of a great damnation?

3. Have you seen that all your reason and the light you have are nothing but darkness? And that you cannot have a saving knowledge of the Father or of His Son, nor can you know yourself either, without the supernatural work of the Holy Spirit in enlightening the eyes of your mind?

4. Have you come to see your inability to think even one good thought, or to perform a single act acceptable to God, without His Spirit to enable you, and that sin has dishonoured you, weakened you and defiled you to such a degree that you cannot raise yourself nor help yourself until God takes the work into His own hands?

5. Have you seen your total need to be clothed in the righteousness of Christ in the presence of God? Do you hate, despise and loathe your own works, your vows, your almsgiving, or any other good in yourself, as a means of your justification, craving with all your heart to be made righteous in His righteousness—regarding this righteousness as the only fountain which is able to cleanse you from all uncleanness?

6. Have you seen your need of faith more than of any other grace, knowing that faith is the hand that receives this eternal righteousness—that it is faith that receives Christ in all His offices—believing in, and embracing all the promises of God—that it is faith that brings the far-off things into the present, and makes things unbelievable to reason to be more substantial than the whole world—have you seen your need of this faith? And that a faith worked by man will not do, but only that which is the work of the Holy Spirit? Has this light and this conviction rooted itself so deeply that it has made you willing to take your leave of all your idols and your loves—all your pleasures, and all the things which before were lovely and dear and precious to you—such as your right eye and your right foot, your sweetest sin, your most secret lust, in order that Christ may be the Head, the King and the Bridegroom of your soul?

7. Have you, as a man does in building a house, counted the cost of withstanding all oppositions, and of suffering all the mockery, persecution, tribulation and afflictions that may come in the cause of the gospel of Christ, and to give your life for it if needs be?

8. Though you have not received the witness of the Spirit, yet are you seeking God with all your heart, and that as a constant disposition of the soul (not in fits or waves of conviction), longing to lay hold on God, wanting nothing else but Him alone, and counting all things loss that you may gain Him, not resting till you possess Him?

9. Can you rest short of a true knowledge that Christ is in you, and that you know that you truly believe, so that you have such a view of

the righteousness of Christ satisfying the justice of God on your behalf, that it kindles in you a love for Him, and urges you to obedience?

10. What is it that is urging you to join us—is it the necessity for more light, for more instruction and direction in the things of God? Are you coming to us because you believe that God is with us, and that you too will receive some blessings in our company? Is there, to any degree, a false purpose leading you to us? Has a coldness come between you and some other congregation, so that you flee to us for refuge and safety?

11. Are you willing to take rebukes and chastening and instruction from us, so long as we do all these things in the sight of the Lord?

12. Will you refrain from repeating to the ungodly world any of the things that we discuss here between ourselves, as that would be casting them to the swine?

13. Are you willing to give rebukes as well as to receive them, and to use every gift that you possess to promote the Lord's work in our midst?

14. Will you be generous in contributing as much as you possibly can to help the poor members of this fellowship?

EUSEBIUS: Is it not suitable for anyone who has a leading, to ask his question of the man seeking membership?

THEOPHILUS: Yes, it is; and very profitable, for as there is safety in the multiplicity of counsellors, so, through a variety of questions, will the true state of things be elicited. It is customary in the Sessions to have counsel for any important case, many of them questioning and cross-questioning in order to arrive at the truth, and it is more necessary in the religious experience societies for several men to seek for evidences of grace in the man seeking membership, or to disabuse his mind about the eternal state of his soul. But let those who do the questioning take care that one does not hinder another by speaking two at a time, or by asking too many questions, so that the man is not able to answer them, because the questioning itself will become confused, or else muddle the one being questioned.

EUSEBIUS: Is it not a good thing to ascertain the mind of the whole fellowship before admitting a man to membership?

THEOPHILUS: A very good thing; and so it is profitable to seek the opinion of all the members on his behaviour from the time he made a profession of religion, especially his neighbours' opinion, in order to know what friends he associates with now. How diligent is he in attending the means of grace? Has any change been noticed in his behaviour in his own home and in the bosom of his own family? Does he seem sanguine or wounded in spirit? And does he in every way show signs that he has in his heart the working of grace?

EUSEBIUS: In the event of a failure to accept the experiences, convictions and evidences of grace in the man who seeks to be received, what should then be done in such a case?

THEOPHILUS: Either he must be rejected out of hand—which is very difficult to do—or he may be received on trial. With regard to a flat rejection, we have no basis in Scripture for doing so, unless it is obvious that his life is unworthy and reveals that the truth is not in him; or it transpires that it is for some false purpose that he wants to come into the fellowship; or that he only attends the means of grace in fits and starts, under the turbulent convictions of natural conscience. If these things are not true of him, then, however weak the signs of grace may be in him, if he shows any sign that he has a true desire, and the brethren have had proof of this, and if he is found to hold fast diligently and faithfully to the means of grace, and to hold fast also to the company of the brethren—having left his old habits, and changed his old friendships, his old talk and his old purposes, and showing a newness of life and of behaviour to all his neighbours—however feeble the signs of grace in him, I say, as long as he pursues such a new way of life and behaviour as this, he has the invitation of the gospel in the Old Testament and the New: 'Ho, everyone that thirsteth, come ye to the waters, and he that hath no money; come ye, buy and eat; yea, come, buy wine and milk without money and without price.' Again, 'A bruised reed shall he not break, and the smoking flax shall he not quench.' And again, 'And let him that is athirst come. And whosoever will, let him take the water of life freely.' Therefore, no one in the person of a seeker, and with a true desire for eternal life, should be shut out, however faint may be the revelations and visitations of God to him.

EUSEBIUS: But what is your procedure for putting a person 'on trial'?

THEOPHILUS: The usual way for one who wants to become a member of the fellowship is for him to give his name to the stewards of the society some time beforehand; and for such stewards then to question him privately, and that on more than one occasion, also to ask his neighbours about him, and to ask some of his friends what difference they see in him, and to make a point of getting an account of him from the lips of the godly and the ungodly as far as possible; and when a month or two is spent on this enquiry into the reality of his state of grace—that is what is called a 'trial'. Then, if the stewards find him fit to come before the entire body of the fellowship, let every one question him as we said previously, asking for the testimony of all the members as to his being in a true state of grace, and let him be received—if counted worthy—by the consent of the entire fellowship.

EUSEBIUS: When he is received like this, is there any charge given him to abide by the rules, the discipline and the principles of the fellowship? And if there is, who should give it?

THEOPHILUS: The charge is given by whomsoever has the suitable gifts to do so, and perhaps two or three will give them—one remembering one thing, and another remembering another thing; but the substance of the charge is, to all intents and purposes, what we have already said, namely that they should not cast pearls before swine—not tell the secrets of the church to an ungodly world, nor recount the weaknesses, the troubles, and the trials of the saints to the dogs who would hold up to ridicule the things that trouble the Church of God; they should not fraternize with the ungodly world except through force of circumstance, but keep as close as possible to the company of the truly godly people, taking and also giving correction meekly and humbly, the one as well as the other—and living in love with the entire society, not loving the ones who rebuke and chasten one jot less than those who comfort; charging them too that they should be conscientious about attending services, and to refrain from empty talk and from carrying gossip about one member to another, so helping to stop all jealousy, prejudice, hostility and envy in any of the members; but by all possible means, by word and deed, to kindle in all a love for each other; watching not only over his own life but also over the lives of his fellow-members; and whenever he should find in them anything wrong, to rebuke them privately and to hide their faults from the brethren; to observe whether such an one will take a private warning, and forsake his fault; and if he does not, then to bring this fault to the attention of one of the stewards; and if that does not have the desired effect, to bring him before two or three of them; and if this fails, to bring him before the entire fellowship. These, and other things like this, constitute the kind of charge that some gifted members of the society should give to those who are received into membership.

V

How to deal with the older members of the fellowship—is it best to catechize them?—if so, the questions that must be put to them, as, for instance, with regard to their witness—their growing awareness of the deceit of their heart—their growth in love to the church—the tenderness of their consciences—their deadness to self-will—their motives in every religious work—the use they are making of the talents they have received—a word on the special counsel to be given on some occasions, instead of catechizing—the nature of such counselling to meet the special circumstances of the fellowship.

EUSEBIUS: And now, tell me a little about the existing members of the church—is it right to catechize these, or not? And if it is necessary, how should they be questioned?

THEOPHILUS: It may be that some of these will speak without being questioned, and this is the best way, if any of them should be moved to do this, because it gives delight and enjoyment when a man of his own free will gives some account of the works of the Spirit of grace and manifestations of the love of God on his soul, or, on the other hand, of the depths of Satan's temptations, the straitening and the bondage of the spirit, or any such pressures on the soul. This is much better than having to ask questions of men spiritually dull and cold, with little knowledge of God or of their own hearts; for one will only waste time with them without receiving any enlightenment or edification. But, if one must ask questions of these members of longer standing, they could be somewhat as follows:

(1) As to the clarity of their witness—how did they first receive their witness? And have they lost any of it since they first received it? What was the effect wrought in them by this witness? Has this witness been repeated by the Holy Spirit, or have they never received it since? And do they now believe that their sins are forgiven; and that Christ has died for them in particular; that God has loved them with an everlasting love? And does the Holy Spirit bear witness with their spirit that they are children of God? Do they possess these things? Or do they only have feelings of hope engendered by the enjoyment and pleasure that they get from hearing the Word, and from various other religious exercises when they are met together with the saints, but which they then lose when they are by themselves? And, further, when great tempests of unbelief beat upon them, where do they turn—to this old experience, or to Christ

Himself, to seek for new light and a new experience, as well as for wisdom and strength?

(2) Are they conscious of more spiritual light within, revealing to them more of the purity of the law, the holiness of God, the plague of their own hearts, the evil of sin, the preciousness of the righteousness of Christ, and all the promises of the New Covenant, together with the innumerable wiles of the world, the flesh and the devil to lure them away from God?

(3) Is their love increasing toward the church? Do they sympathize more with her in all her trials; have they a less censorious spirit towards those who fall; have they greater compassion for all, feeling the troubles and afflictions of others as though they were suffering them themselves?

(4) Is their conscience more tender to convict them of the very first beginnings of sin in the mind, such as the first beginnings of a bitter nature, a careless spirit, an intemperate care for the things of this world, of envy, suspicion, pride, conceit, lasciviousness, or any other corruption that it sees insinuating itself like a serpent, and poisoning the whole man? Are they also being convicted of things that the world calls innocent—such as the idle word, the foolish talking, jesting and gossiping about the things of this world, greed of gain, desire to walk out and about in order to be seen and to see others, and such like things that spring from a light spirit and an unbroken heart?

(5) What new lessons has the Lord taught them of late? Do they see more of the evil of unbelief, the deceit of their heart, the wiles of the devil, the lure of sin, the delusions of the world? Do they see that they are ever in peril without the strength of Christ to empower them, and are they learning to lean more upon Him for strength, wisdom, and understanding to enable them to walk through such great dangers to the eternal world?

(6) As they examine themselves carefully, do they find that they are growing in grace, and are nearer heaven than they were at the beginning? And if they are growing, what is their growth like? Is it that they see more purity, more good inclinations, heavenly virtues, and holiness in themselves, or that they see a greater need of leaning on Christ and trusting Him for strength, power, righteousness, wisdom and sanctification?

(7) Do they examine their motives in whatever they take in hand to do, whether it is for the glory of God, or for gain, pleasure, comfort, praise or some other satisfaction for themselves?

(8) By whose will do they walk and do all the things that they do? Is it by the will of God in His Word, or by their own will? Do they search the Word carefully, to know His will in order to perform it; do

they in prayer lay the matter before the Lord, afraid of going before Him or of lagging behind Him, or of doing anything without knowing His mind in the matter?

(9) Are they making use of the talents which they have received from God—their learning, their memory, their gifts, their bodies, their souls, together with their wealth and their time, altogether bent on glorifying the Lord and building up and edifying His church?

These, and others like them, are the questions that should be put to those who are of longer standing in religion, in order that they may add to their faith virtue, and to virtue knowledge, and to knowledge temperance, and to temperance patience, and to patience godliness, and to godliness brotherly kindness, and to brotherly kindness charity; that they may be perfected in every good work. But understand this: though the above rules are all good if they are used in the wisdom and the Spirit of the Lord, yet without the accompaniment of His beloved authority they are nothing; therefore the chief duty of those responsible for the societies is to keep a spirit of light and heavenly feeling in them, lest at any time rules and regulations should engender deadness and formality; while striving with all their might to keep out as far as possible every careless spirit, unbroken heart, lovelessness, prejudice, envy, evil whispers, a gossiping spirit and everything else that could engender coldness between the members.

EUSEBIUS: What if, at times, neither catechizing, nor singing, nor praying has any success, but the majority are left dead, dry, and in spiritual darkness in spite of all these good efforts—what should be done then?

THEOPHILUS: You must understand that sometimes especial exhortations may be given to religious fellowships, which are as profitable as the catechizing, and, indeed, to some types of people and at certain times, much more so; especially when a visiting preacher comes to a private fellowship, he being highly gifted and many people having come together, with some, possibly, from other fellowships. Because, between shyness, pride and the unusual circumstances, many will be too bashful and nervous to answer the kind of questions that the illustrious stranger might ask them; and because of this it would be better for him to give them some general advice that would be instrumental in edifying them in doctrine, in spirit and in conduct worthy of the faith.

And very often this type of special counselling will be more acceptable to all, and will be less likely to disturb the spirit of the brethren than the public catechizing, because, in the first place, it is very difficult to find men who are willing to speak honestly of their spiritual state before so many people, especially among the strangers, with a stranger also doing the questioning. Secondly, if whoever is being questioned begins partly to hide his true state, telling one side of the story and concealing the other, he will get deeper and deeper into difficulties and find himself finally tangled in a wilderness, not knowing how to get out of it, and, with shame, will have to relapse into silence. In the third place, if this stranger who is catechizing is not satisfied with the people being questioned, he will nurse hard thoughts of them, without rightly understanding their state, and this will disturb the man himself, so that instead of being edified he will from there on nurse a bitterness and coldness towards the fellowship.

EUSEBIUS: What are these special lessons and counsels?

THEOPHILUS: Such as the case demands. Sometimes, through the pride of arrogant men who are all for bringing in some new light, false doctrines eat like a canker in a religious community; and these false doctrines make such headway, and with such approval and light, that it looks as though no one could gainsay them; but in such a case it is a good thing to prove the true doctrines of faith from Holy Scripture, and to free the brethren from an erring spirit and from heresies, and with all gentleness to draw them back to the right path.

Again, if a religious community has gone astray in pursuing a life of licence, pleasure and wantonness, it is a good thing to utter grave and authoritative rebukes against such a torrent of natural passions, showing from Scripture how difficult it is 'for those who were once enlightened, and have tasted of the heavenly gift, and were made partakers of the Holy Ghost, and have tasted the good word of God, and the powers of the world to come, if they shall fall away'—to pleasures, the lusts of the flesh and the enticements of nature—'to renew them again unto repentance; seeing they crucify to themselves the Son of God afresh . . .'. But the preacher should take great care to censure more severely those who take the lead in these errors, than those who are only beginning to be led astray by them. As the Apostle Jude says, 'And of some have compassion, making a difference: And others save with fear, pulling them out of the fire; hating even the garment spotted by the flesh' (Jude 22, 23).

But if there are none of these things needing to be spoken against, perhaps it would be good to give advice against laziness of spirit, lukewarmness, lack of fruit, and neglect of the gathering of themselves together, which things are often found in the various religious fellowships; or else, if the community is warm and lively and full of zeal, yet it would be good to exhort them to show all the fruits congruous with that zeal and heavenly warmth to the world outside, as it were, to conduct themselves honestly, meekly and humbly, never using craft or deceit, fraud or lie, nor any behaviour unworthy of those professing the gospel of Christ; but rather such as answers perfectly to the character that Christ and the Apostles give to true believers. And urging them also to show such fruits of the church of God as will encourage in them love, compassion, sympathy, gentleness, a forgiving spirit, hiding of (others') faults, a love of doing kindnesses, and generosity.

Here, a gifted preacher can enlarge upon all the duties of the gospel to poor and rich, old and young, the sick and the healthy, relatives and strangers; national duties, and every department of life consonant with holiness. Here, the preacher can show the effects of every grace; he can distinguish between faith and presumption, true repentance and legalistic fear, true love towards God and the moods of flesh and nature, a broken spirit and a melancholy spirit, spiritual joy and presumptuous joy, together with many other states in which grace and nature are so like each other that it needs a discriminating eye to distinguish between them. Through preaching on these matters on occasion to a religious fellowship, they will be taught little by little in all the mysteries of godliness, and such special counselling does completely fulfil the place of catechizing in some circumstances.

VI

The question of keeping strict discipline, putting out of fellowship any leading a loose and unworthy life—instances given in Scripture of showing mercy to some who had fallen—harmony of the Scriptures that seem to be contradictory, with regard to either bearing with or treating harshly those who sin—three kinds of fallen ones, the first to be suffered in the society because of the fierceness of their temptations, and their broken spirit afterwards—the second and third to be put out unless they are swift to show signs of repentance—the aforementioned Scriptures to be expounded and harmonized in these three respects.

EUSEBIUS: Do you not at times have to deal more harshly in discipline, by putting some offenders out of the fellowship when their lives have become loose and undisciplined, full of weaknesses and errors, or if they have fallen into some open sin through the force of temptation, or spiritual carelessness and idleness? That is why I would ask you how to deal with members of the fellowship in such a case. What are the faults for which they should be excommunicated? How far should one bear with them, to allow them to stay in the fellowship when they have trespassed? And again, how should those who are put out be dealt with? Must one be cold, dry, and distant towards them? Or should one seek them out and speak to them, to see whether they are on their feet again after their fall, and whether their wounds are healed and true repentance granted unto them? And also, what signs should one seek in them of a real restoration into communion with God before they are re-admitted into the fellowship?

THEOPHILUS: You have asked me many questions, and I will do my best to give you satisfaction. However others may think in this matter, I am never anxious to put anyone out of the communion of the church of God except for serious and unavoidable reasons, such as seeing a man going on in his sin, loving it, delighting in it, and falling frequently into it without repenting, but rather hardening his heart and despising all convicting feelings aroused by God and by man. But when a believer falls suddenly, with no thought of the sin previously in his mind, but falling into it from the force of the fiery temptation, that came like a hurricane from the frontiers of hell, or as a flood without warning from the mountains of flesh and blood, such should not be cast out in the heat of the moment; but they should be reproved with gentleness, and, while showing them the disgrace and the guilt of their wrongdoing, sympathizing with them and pitying them, and earnestly beseeching them never again to go near to such slippery rocks. And what strengthens me in my judgment is—

(1) The example of our Lord Jesus Himself with His Apostle Peter, who not only denied his Lord, but with disrespectful words about Him cursed and swore that he knew nothing of that Man whom they had taken —that he had never seen Him before, and that he cared not what they would do with Him, confirming this with awful and horrible oaths. Yet, because it was a wild, sudden temptation, and it was only Peter's tongue that denied his Lord, and that also because of great fear; and because he repented immediately, weeping bitterly for his fall, our good Lord received him into the number of His Apostles.

(2) The Scriptures say, 'If a man be overtaken in a fault, ye which are spiritual, restore such an one in the spirit of meekness; considering thyself, lest thou also be tempted' (Galatians 6:1). And you know that to restore in the spirit of meekness is not to cast a man out of the fellowship, but to persuade and entice him by all love, gentleness and affection to acknowledge his fault, and to forsake it from then on and for ever.

(3) We find many hurtful faults in the members of the Asian churches; yet the Holy Spirit did not bid them to be cut out of the body, but threatened them, that if they did not repent of their sins, their candlesticks, that is, their preachers, would be removed from their place; or else, that God would cast them into a bed of great tribulation, except they repent of their sins.

(4) Our Lord's attitude towards the woman taken in adultery shows that the harshness of the Old Testament belongs not at all to the spirit of the New, but that the spirit of the New Covenant says, 'If any man sin'— and sorrows for his sin—'we have an advocate with the Father, Jesus Christ the righteous'; and again, 'Go and sin no more, lest a worse thing befall thee.'

(5) We find in the churches in Corinth many great and hurtful faults, such as going to law before the unbelievers, marrying unbelievers, having divisions among themselves over the preachers of the Word—one taking the part of Paul, another of Peter, yet another on the side of Apollos. And yet it was only for one of their various faults that we find Paul putting a man out of the church, and that was because he had taken his father's wife—that is, either to marry her or to live in sin with her; and to make the matter worse, the church was taking this lightly and as a matter for jesting; or else, from envy or revenge, rejoicing in his fall—

which shows that in that church they were guilty, to an almost unheard of degree, of regarding sinning against the Lord lightly.

EUSEBIUS: I understand that it is better to err on the side of mercy and sympathy than on the side of condemning, killing, and nursing wrath against a believer that has fallen to temptation, for our Lord says, 'Judge not, that ye be not judged. For with what judgment ye judge, ye shall be judged: and with what measure ye mete, it shall be measured to you again. And why beholdest thou the mote that is in thy brother's eye, but considerest not the beam that is in thine own eye? ... Thou hypocrite, first cast out the beam out of thine own eye; and then shalt thou see clearly to cast out the mote out of thy brother's eye' (Matthew 7: 1-3, 5). And without doubt, the best of men should act with fear and trembling when casting a soul out of the church of God, lest the day come when he himself should be put out, as the Apostle says: 'Let him that thinketh he standeth take heed lest he fall' (1 Corinthians 10: 12).

And yet, there are several other Scriptures which bid us not to suffer sin in any, lest, if we should do so, we become guilty with them in their sin, as the Apostle Paul says, 'Be not ye therefore partakers with them' (Ephesians 5: 7). And a second lesson, 'And have no fellowship with the unfruitful works of darkness, but rather reprove them' (Ephesians 5: 11). And the same Apostle says the same thing to Timothy when he bids him to 'lay hands suddenly on no man', lest in so doing he become 'a partaker of other men's sins' (1 Timothy 5: 22). And the Apostle John says in his second Epistle, 'If there come any unto you, and bring not this doctrine' (that is, the doctrine of abiding in the Spirit of Christ, and of holy living) 'receive him not into your house, neither bid him God speed; for he that biddeth him God speed is partaker of his evil deeds'—which warnings give us to understand that the right way for the godfearing is to separate themselves from profane, loose-living and unclean men, however great may be their pretence and profession of religion; and also to cast out such from their assemblies, if they do not hasten to repentance from their evil living and shameful behaviour. And to confirm me still further in this matter, Paul says to the Corinthian church, in his first Epistle, 'I', says he, 'wrote unto you (before) . . . but now I have written unto you (again) not to keep company, if any man that is called a brother be a fornicator, or covetous, or an idolater, or a railer, or a drunkard, or an extortioner; with such an one no not to eat' (1 Corinthians 5: 11)—that is, as I see it, do not make a close friend or a bosom companion of him—do not take pleasure in the company of a man who loves the sweetness of sinful lusts more than he loves God, lest people should suppose that because you sit together, eat together, drink together and spend your time together, you love his ways, and delight in his activities. It is these Scriptures, and others like them, which lead me to believe that church discipline enjoins us to keep away from those who live lives unworthy of the gospel of Christ, and for certain offences to put them out of the church, as the Apostle says, 'For what have I to do to judge them also that are without? do not ye judge them that are within? . . . Therefore put away from among yourselves that wicked person' (1 Corinthians 5: 12, 13).

But here I am at a loss to know when, and to whom, we should show compassion; and towards whom, and when, on the other hand, we should use greater severity; for the Apostle Jude says, 'And of some have compassion, making a difference: And others save with fear, pulling them out of the fire; hating even the garment spotted by the flesh' (Jude 22, 23). Therefore, my dear father in the faith, please reconcile these various Scriptures, which sometimes tell us to show mercy to, and at others to be severe with and to separate ourselves from, those who fall into sin and yet make a profession of godliness.

THEOPHILUS: My beloved, when the Scriptures seem to strike one against the other, understand that the cause for this is the darkness of our understanding, and that there is not, in reality, a single inconsistency in the Holy Scriptures; and the only thing for us to do (whenever we find anything obscure) is to run to the Lord for heavenly light; for the same Spirit that wrote the Word is the only One who can open out the Word which He Himself gave to His Church as a pillar of fire and of cloud to lead her unto life. But in order to follow the instructions of the various Scriptures which you have quoted, which seem to be contradicting each other, there are several things to consider in the matter of disciplining those who walk unworthy of the gospel of Christ.

First of all, understand the case of a man falling into some public sin: if it is for the first time—if, from the force of some trial such as persecution, imprisonment or want, he be overcome by fear; if, from failure to recognise the lust that enticed him, he, never having had any previous experience of it should fall blindly, not seeing the hidden snare laid by the world and Satan to catch his soul unawares—in such a case it is good to show compassion, to rebuke him gently, and to raise him up again to his rightful place with all tenderness and gentleness, especially if he is sick and sorrowful in spirit for having brought disgrace on the way of the Lord; and the Scripture that bears this out says, 'Brethren, if a man be overtaken in a fault, ye which are spiritual, restore such an one in the spirit of meekness; considering thyself, lest thou also be tempted' (Galatians 6: 1). And another Scripture says, 'If any man see his brother sin a sin which is not unto death, he shall ask, and he shall give him life for them that sin not unto death' (1 John 5: 16).

Secondly, if, however, he who professes religion has fallen to the same fault again and again, and that with very little provocation, and with every sign that he has never hated his fault, but loves it and fondles it in secret, so that he does not sorrow for it, but rather shows nothing but an empty, hypocritical pretence, springing more from the shame that the disgrace has caused him, than from pain for having sinned against a merciful and gracious God—it is necessary to discipline such an one as this before all, as a warning, an alarm and a cause of fear to others; and if the sin is against the law of the land, and is known to the world outside, it is profitable to lay upon the guilty some public or open punishment or rebuke, so that the world may come to recognize the fact that the church of God does not suffer any to live in any sin. This may be done either by excommunicating the man from the fellowship, or in some other way. And with this agrees the Scripture which says, 'Them that sin rebuke before all, that others also may fear' (1 Timothy 5: 20).

In the *third* place, if one who professes religion (though he has not fallen to fornication, drunkenness, fighting, murder, stealing and all the other sins about which the world cries out), yet is living the same kind of life as the ungodly world—finding his friends among those who are friends of the world; walking according to the course of the world; using illegal ways in business; wanton; indulging in empty vain talk, drinking and gluttony; if he is proud, lying, envious, malicious, given to all licentious behaviour, without a sign of regret or pain for any outrage that he is responsible for—the duty of the fellowship is to rebuke such an one sharply and with authority, threatening to cast him out from the communion of the saints. And if he does not improve his way of life, and that speedily, and give clear indications of a broken and wounded spirit, it is right to cast him out in the name of the Lord. And with this the Scripture agrees, which says, 'And others save with fear, pulling them out of the fire; hating even the garment spotted by the flesh' (Jude 23).

EUSEBIUS: What is to be done to those who leave the fellowship of their own free will, having once entered it in much warmth, love and life, but who have either been enticed by some lust, such as carnal love, love of the world, or some natural pleasure, or else have in some way grown cold towards every good thing, and in the end have lost all taste for any of the means of grace? If they listen at all, it is only by some chance, as it were; and if they come to the experience meeting, they are there in fear, and ill at ease; but it is a very uncommon thing to see them wend their way to any such place. How should we behave toward these?

THEOPHILUS: They have departed from God, and that is why they have departed from you; and it would be a matter of great joy to win them back again; for, whoever could do that, the Scripture says of him that he will 'shine . . . as the stars for ever and ever' (Daniel 12: 3). For this reason it is your duty, first and foremost, to pray for them, that God will restore them to Himself; and then to talk often with them in a fair and courteous manner, persuading them to return from the error of their ways; showing them the awful peril of backsliding—the double damnation that awaits those who depart from God; drawing their attention to the awe-inspiring Scriptures that deal with the backslider, such as, 'For it is impossible for those who were once enlightened, and have tasted of the heavenly gift, and were made partakers of the Holy Ghost, and have tasted the good word of God, and the powers of the world to come, if they shall fall away, to renew them again unto repentance; seeing they crucify to themselves the Son of God afresh, and put him to an open shame' (Hebrews 6: 4-6); showing them too the Scripture that saith, 'For if we sin wilfully after that we have received the knowledge of the truth, there remaineth no more sacrifice for sins, but a certain fearful looking for of judgment and fiery indignation, which shall devour the adversaries' (Hebrews 10: 26, 27). And perhaps, by the earnest, importunate prayers of the fellowship on their behalf (for the effectual fervent prayer of the righteous availeth much); by loving them, following them from place to place, giving them no peace in their backsliding; by pleading with them with all tenderness, gentleness and love that they would cleave anew to the Lord, it may please the merciful and gracious God to restore them to the faith, and to crown those who were instrumental in bringing this excellent task to a successful end.

VII

Concerning the things that are not suitable to be mentioned in the society, such as, wandering and blasphemous thoughts; sudden, transitory, fiery temptations in the mind; secret lapses, when true repentance follows them; our corrupt lives, before receiving grace; the faults and failings of others—other things that are suitable to speak of, such as, things that pertain more to the spirit than to the body—such things as will enlighten the entire society as to the state of a soul—things that are able to save them from being downtrodden by our spiritual enemies—the inner convictions and sufferings as the result of sin—the graces and heavenly frames that God works in us—the disappointments we suffer in ourselves—and finally, everything that kindles love in one toward another—instructions to the stewards of the society on how to behave in their general conduct, their discretion and readiness to protect and keep the counsel and secrets of the society—concerning alms, to whom the money of the society is to be distributed—the disorder that often arises from this matter—who are the widows indeed, who are the fitting recipients of the collections and gifts of the fellowship, together with various thoughts regarding too high living among preachers and other professing Christians.

EUSEBIUS: There was some talk between us at the beginning of our conversation about the imprudence that might obtain in meetings of this kind, on several considerations, and especially in one way, that is, through young people saying more of what is unfitting and unprofitable for themselves and others, and possibly less of other things that would be edifying; and how the zeal of such young people might drive them on into the error on the one hand of saying too much, in the same way as the lukewarmness of the older members might make them on the other hand say too little. But I forgot at that time to follow up my question, and you began to speak of the stewards of the society; but it still weighs on me to ask, What things may be said, and what things should not be said in such meetings? Because, as I said, there could at times be a real lack of wisdom in this matter. For as young oxen who have never before been under the yoke often fail to keep a straight furrow, but pull wildly from one side to the other, giving a great deal of trouble to others, and much more trouble to themselves than they need, spoiling the regularity of ridges and furrows; so the babes who have newly come to taste the delights of the things of God are ready to run to one side or the other of the straight path—either the depth of conviction on the one hand, driving them to tell of every evil deed, every deceit, and every uncleanness they had ever committed; or else a taste of the spirit of freedom on the other hand, setting them off to tell of every sweet thought, every delightful dream, and every comfortable opinion which they have of themselves, with little substance in it all. For this reason, in such a mixed fellowship of men and women, old and young, youths and maidens, I am afraid that, on the one hand, too much of the truth may be withheld, or, on the other hand, too much may be spoken; which, either way, must be very harmful to the edification of the fellowship.

THEOPHILUS: That is quite true, and some churches have gone astray as the members have told too much of their corruption, their uncleanness, their treachery, their dishonesty, their unchastity, and all the accursedness that was in them before receiving grace; and, as you said, so much so that great disgrace was brought on the ways of the Lord, and the ministers of those churches had to make a rule from that time on, that none should tell of particular things relating to themselves in the days before they came to make a profession of faith, lest by doing so they would have to lay open the sins of others with their own, or also have to reveal things about themselves which would mean everlasting shame for them and for their children, or possibly some things that might cause separation and division in families, congregations and even in general society.

Because of this, my opinion is that there are various matters that should be avoided in the fellowship of the brethren, even when among our dearest friends. In the *first* place, the aweful and terrible blasphemous thoughts that Satan insinuates into our spirits. Nature has practically no hand in these: they belong to the devil; they are in his own image and likeness—to wit, hating God, despising Him, querying all His attributes, being jealous and envious of Him, and trampling His greatness underfoot. These things are the office, the element and the pleasure of this angel of despair, and he drives them into the spirits of the godly in order to trouble them, to confuse them, to disturb their spirits, and to destroy, if he could, their love for and their peace with the Lord. These things are like lightning, striking into a room and putting everyone in great fear; yet it was not produced by anything in the room, but by the poisonous sulphur in the atmosphere. In the same way, it is not our corruption, great though it is, that is the cause of these blasphemous thoughts, but Satan; and it is he who will be punished for such temptations, for our spirit has not consented to them, and we do not need to feel guilty about them, nor to be disturbed by them, nor to nurse one grain of doubt because they come to us, for they are often the portion of some of the noblest of the saints. And, indeed, it is not good for us to talk about them, lest they should multiply by our doing so, or have an effect upon others; and, besides, they are too terrible and aweful to be repeated; but the duty of all who are suffering temptations such as these is to pray fervently against them.

Secondly, it is not a good thing to relate the stray, wandering thoughts that run into our spirits like a river in flood: doubtless these stem from a careless heart and an idle spirit; but if they were all to be related, there would have to be as much time given to the repeating of them as was given to the receiving of them in the first place—a whole day given to the repeating of the wandering thoughts of another day, even if they could all be remembered! But oh! what multitudes of them are devoid of any substance, and what multitudes more pertain to things not fit to be repeated! Some to do with fear, some with carnal confidence; some with love, some with hate; some with sorrow, some with joy; some with wishing for certain things, some with hatred of other things; and multitudes without number to do with desires for the world, or with discontent in it, or desires for respect and gain, for ease and earthly glory. And there is hardly a commandment, from the beginning of the Old Testament to the end of the New, that is not broken in wandering thoughts, so that it is a hundred times better to repeat these wild, destructive, and, in the end, stinking thoughts (like the locusts of Egypt) to God, rather than to men, for fear that they might misunderstand them, and suppose that these thoughts are rooted and permanent in the very depth of the heart of the man who related them; whereas they were in reality only what Satan was throwing in to fill and to divert the heart that was empty of the presence of the Lord.

Thirdly, it is not a good thing to relate every wild temptation that comes to arouse our passions, when it does not last long, nor is willingly received. There is a difference between temptations presented to the mind, and a wandering mind. The first come with persistent force and authority, upon some one part of the soul—on the understanding, or the will, or one of the passions of the soul, moving that passion to inordinate affection for a time or to malicious hatred, to presumptuous confidence or craven fear, to rejoice immoderately or to speak as one without hope, to covet unreasonably or to hate unto utter abhorrence; and all this persisting with force upon the spirit for quite some time. But a stray thought is only something that floats on the surface, and changes from one thing to another in a minute, so that oftentimes a hundred thoughts will lodge in the soul in the space of an hour. And as it is not a good thing to report these, so it is not a good thing to report the temptations just mentioned—with some exceptions, namely, those that have a controlling influence on the soul—that cannot be dislodged by praying, listening, reading and meditating, but cleave constantly to the affections, and seem likely to quench the fire of the love of the Lord. But as for those of them that are of short duration, that yield to prayer, or that do not militate against the presence of the Lord, it is better not to recount these in the religious fellowship, lest they should happen to deal with love to some, hatred to others, prejudice, envy, jealousy, or some contempt, dishonour, and coldness of spirit towards some truly godly and respected men; or they (the short-lived temptations) may concern desire, lust and lasciviousness, and so be very harmful to others in many respects. Therefore, in such a case, it is better to tell them to God than to men.

Fourthly, as you have already partly intimated, it is not a good thing to tell of our old erroneous ways before we came to know the Lord —it serves no good purpose to relate all the various abominable things that God has forgiven, that the world has forgotten, from which our own consciences have been cleansed, and which God chooses not to remember. Perhaps in time this might do great harm to our own good name, and to our children after us; to our usefulness in the church, and possibly to our interest; and perhaps as much harm, or more, to our neighbours also, such as bringing calumny on some, loss to others, affecting adversely the life of some, and bringing trouble and ill-health to others; for, by reporting various sins that we committed in a state of nature, we must often report the sins of those who were consenting with us at that time in drunkenness, strife, deceit, dishonesty, lasciviousness—which, when revealed openly, could bring coldness into a marriage, cause division in families, cause disturbances, breed prejudice, arouse envy and malice, and set district and church together by the ears.

Fifthly, it is not a good thing either to tell of our every lapse, and how the God of mercy lifted us on to our feet and rekindled His gift in us. We are no better for sounding abroad our weaknesses to others, lest some who hear us may be so narrow in their judgment and so dark in their understanding of the doctrines of grace that they suppose that a man who has received grace never falls to temptation; and for that reason they will have doubts about those who have thus fallen into any sin, and will be prejudiced against them and will put restraints upon them, though they have been honest enough to confess their faults to their fellow members. And again, evil consequences might follow the relating of lapses that God has hidden, and for which the believers have received forgiveness, and a contrite heart given them as a result of this— namely, that others might take advantage from this, to withstand the same kind of temptation less firmly when it comes to meet them; and above all, lest those who have fallen in this way, by telling of their fall, should make themselves less useful in their various gifts of catechizing, singing, praising, praying, rebuking, reproving, comforting and edifying their fellow pilgrims, through their lapses being brought to the remembrance of these, and they become cold towards them, and all their gifts become useless. But although God has thus forgiven them, and hidden their faults a hundred times, yet it is their duty to confess them to God and to sorrow for them a thousand and ten thousand times. For this reason we find in the Scriptures many of the saints of old, patriarchs and prophets, complaining about the innumerable corruptions of their hearts, and yet concealing the nature of these corruptions. David says that he had kept himself from his sin, but he does not tell us what that sin was that tended most frequently to beset him. Paul, too, speaks of a thorn in the flesh: he does not tell us whether this thorn was something painful or some corruption, but he does say that it was a messenger of Satan. Therefore, as I have said, to tell of every slip, every weakness, every error, and every occasion when we have lost our way, to a fellowship full of professors of religion, is not fitting, in case we have cause to regret it later.

In the *sixth* place, it is not a good thing to complain much about others in these fellowship meetings; bringing complaints against others often stems from a self-righteous spirit, lamenting over some bitter strokes of providence, or a secret grudge against those who once did us harm; therefore there should be no complaints in the experience meeting, except such as are really necessary, and especially should husbands never bring complaints against their wives, nor wives against their husbands. Marriage is such a close relationship that, whichever partner finds fault, it must be that he is finding fault with his own flesh, for they two shall be one flesh, and it is usually found that the faults of the one lie at the door of the other.

EUSEBIUS: Tell me further, I beseech you, what things are most suitable to be related in this type of meeting, when lack of wisdom and a hot zeal have, unconsciously, done so much harm.

THEOPHILUS: There is none but the great God, through His Spirit, that can direct children to walk in a way that they know not, and yet not go astray; and as He led ancient Israel of old with His pillar of fire by night and His cloud by day, so has He promised for His own people that though they be fools they shall not err. But the instruments whereby all things are kept decent and in order are the stewards of the society, who should—as we said at the beginning—in catechizing, ask only about those things which are meet and suitable to be repeated and confessed, and to this end also they should stop zealous young men in their confessions, as soon as they see that they are going too far; and for that matter, the substance of your question has already been answered, when we showed the kind of question that should be put to young people; for the answers to those questions are the things that should be said by them.

But yet, as the Apostle says, 'To speak the same thing to me is not grievous, but for you it is safe'; therefore

(1) Let all things that are said by anyone there (*i.e.* in the meeting) tend more to the things of the soul than to the things of the flesh. The experience meetings have been set up for this purpose, and it follows that the emphasis of the work should be on the state of the soul, and so the Apostle says, 'But exhort one another daily, while it is called today; lest any of you be hardened through the deceitfulness of sin.' The things meant for discussion in these fellowships are the things to awaken consciences, to arouse convictions, to generate zeal, to create a godly fear, to promote love towards God and His church, to reveal sin, and to display the length and the breadth, the depth and the height of the love of Christ which is beyond all knowledge.

(2) Let the answers be such as will show the state of the one being questioned in a clear light to the entire fellowship, so that all may perceive him in that light, to understand his spirit, to know where he stands, whether he is under heavy convictions or light; whether he is under the law or under grace; whether he is a slave to his sins or a brave warrior for the Lord who will take the kingdom of heaven by force; whether he has a right arm not yet cut off or a right eye not yet plucked out. If, having been questioned by all, his position is made as clear as daylight, the entire fellowship may now take pity on him, sympathize with him, counsel him, rebuke him; or, if he is enjoying the presence of the Lord, having come into the fellowship to drink of the good things of the gospel and to taste the sweetness of heavenly things, they may, on the other hand, rejoice together with him with an endless joy, and he will be to them an illustration and a fresh example of the goodness and kindness of God to His church; and since such fellowships as these are established in order to rejoice with them that do rejoice, and to weep with them that weep, then it is necessary to have a clear and open view of people's condition, in order to deal impartially with their immortal souls.

(3) It is necessary to say things that will be helpful to bring us out from under the feet of our enemies, to break our fetters, to relieve us of our burdens, to release our spirits from bondage, guilt and the fear of death, and to bring us to the true liberty of the children of God; and

if we do not speak in these religious fellowships of such things as are likely, with heaven's blessing, to produce a bolder, more confident and more constant spirit in the fight against the flesh, the world and Satan, then one of the objects of our gathering of ourselves together is wasted; and it follows that it is harmful for any to speak here anything in a careless, hard, envious or prejudiced spirit, lest by doing so they kindle bitterness, strife and coldness in the society, and breed reserve, suspicions and bad feeling between one and another. There should always be a fear here of saying anything, except it be in the Spirit of the Lord, the words accompanied by the breath of heaven, so that it might be said that it was the voice of God, and all the people, as one man, assenting to it, and one spirit, like a mighty rushing wind, moving the entire society either to love and rejoicing, or to grief and sorrow of spirit. Therefore, it is not right for one to speak when another is speaking, for it is disorder and confusion for two to speak at the same time; therefore, show respect for each other in the matter of speaking—listen attentively, praying with all your heart that everything may proceed in simplicity, honesty and the fear of the Lord. For one of the chief purposes that believers should have in meeting together and relating their trials and temptations and their troubles, and their many weaknesses, is that they may gain more strength against them and resignation under them, to suffer, and to carry their cross contentedly and with heavenly peace; and if our speaking of these things should turn out to be harmful to ourselves or to others, by hardening some in their lapses or by making others weaker under their trials, or by breeding a narrow, cold and prejudiced spirit in others, there is no doubt but that such handling of the experience meeting is not profitable, nor is it carried on according to the pattern.

(4) It is a good thing to tell of the convictions and inward suffering for sin which the Holy Spirit works in us when we sin; for to give an account of our sins without telling of this is a harmful fault and could encourage people to sin more. The work of the Spirit of grace in convicting, rebuking, and grieving the spirit of the religious professor for his words, his thoughts, his actions and his purposes, is a good sign of the reality of grace; and to relate this sorrow of spirit frequently produces a very good effect on the spirits of others, and produces more of godly fear in the entire fellowship—fear of taking licence to any sin, as they consider the pain, the guilt, and the grievous darkness suffered by the sinning brother or sister as a result of saying or doing according to their desire and their own will.

(5) It is a good thing also to tell of the graces, the heavenly feelings and the sweet delight that the Spirit of life produces in you from time to

time—the answers which you get to your prayers—the promises that God gives you when under trial—the unexpected deliverances you have experienced from things that you fear—the powerful light that you receive in hours of darkness—together with the various times of refreshing from the presence of the Lord which you receive from the preaching of the Word, in prayer, or from some other heavenly ordinance. It is absolutely necessary, I say, that these things be stated and set forth, clearly and with warmth, in the fellowship, for the purpose of getting others to strive for the same things, and in order that all the believers gathered there should praise and bless God for His unspeakable goodness.

(6) It is profitable for you to reveal the shortcomings and disappointments that you find in yourselves; and to let the entire fellowship know that you see yourselves as ever weaker, more ignorant, and more feeble, and increasingly in need of a Mediator who is full of all goodness, grace and righteousness. This self-denying spirit shown in speaking thus will breed more love, compassion, sympathy, and unity among the members, and will break down and banish all jealousy, prejudice, and any coldness of spirit which one may harbour against another. But, lastly, take great care always to speak only those things that will kindle love in the one to the other—things likely to be profitable in weakening interest in the world, the flesh and Satan, and to make the name of the Lord Jesus dearer to each member of the fellowship, so that when you take your leave of one another, you part in warmth and unity, in love and sincere sympathy.

EUSEBIUS: Henceforth I will trouble you no more, my dear and honoured teacher, but will put into practice all the means that you have named—the precious rules, and orders and disciplines that you have set before me, hoping for a blessing upon them, for you have given me much light on things which were obscure to me; and again, as you said, I will wait upon the Lord, for He alone can lead us to the means of grace that He Himself will bless. I see that it is not good to cling too much to one form or order, for it is by doing this that several churches known to me have erred greatly—namely, by following a cold, dead order, and so clinging to it that no one can entice them from it, as though it were some form that the Lord had commanded from His own lips, whereas in truth it is nothing but a form they received from their forefathers, and that a very indifferent form too. But it is a delight to follow God, be it through what means soever that He Himself shall honour. Now, I will go home, and will render thanks for the thought that first struck me, to come to you, believing that the instructions you have given me will be a blessing to me, and to the little fellowship to which I belong; and I will plead with my heavenly Father that you too will not be without your full reward—a hundred blessings in this world, and a thousand in the world to come. And I will not presume to ask any more of you, since I have received my expectations in full, other than your fervent prayers before the great Throne; remember me and my little society; they, like me, are nothing but feeble weaklings, and Satan is old and cunning, temptations are frequent, hidden snares are set on every path, so that only the power and light of heaven can keep us in the midst of such a wilderness, where ten thousand have gone astray, and thousands have fallen never to rise again. But all my comfort in these matters is that heavenly wisdom is mightier than the temptations of Satan, and that God has said in His Word—'The wayfaring men, though fools, shall not err therein.'

THEOPHILUS: You are no happier that you came to me than I am of your coming, for I believe that the Lord sent you, and I now leave you to the care of high heaven and to the Spirit of the Lord, who is able to bless you with all manner of blessings; and although it is so difficult to be the leader of a large number of people of varying ages, standing, and worldly ranks, and especially with varying temperaments, passions and temptations; nevertheless, that same God, who has promised that His people, though fools, shall not err, shall teach you to do all to the glory of His own blessed Name, and for their own eternal good.

But do you on your part take some few words of advice from me, that may be profitable in the hour of trial, since I understand that you (like an elder and a father among children) are a steward and a minister in their midst, going in and out among them, and are the one on whom they lean for enlightenment and instruction in all matters. Therefore,

(1) Be mindful to set good examples before them on all occasions by your life and seemly conduct, behaving courteously, tenderly, patiently and lovingly toward them and all men: never be heated, bitter or confusing—never impatient, grumbling and difficult to handle; but always humble, self-denying, ready to teach the ignorant, and to listen to the complaint of the oppressed and afflicted.

(2) Be mindful to keep to yourself that which is told you. If the steward of the society is a gossip and reveals the secrets of those undergoing trials, who is going to entrust him with their secret matters? Everyone will be afraid of him, lest that which they have whispered in his ear—in their great distress—should be spread abroad throughout the world, and sounded like a trumpet from sea to sea. The priests of the church of Rome, who receive the confessions of all the people, from

the king to the chimney sweep, are able to keep the secrets of the church as long as they live; and if an adulterous church can do this, how much greater is the duty of the true church to keep what she is given to keep! And if the stewards of a society cannot be trusted to keep secrets, it is better to tell the secrets to that God who is able both to keep them and to forgive them too. There are many things that godly men want to discuss with their teachers in private, that cannot be mentioned except to some one person, and he must be such that not a word concerning it will ever pass his lips again—a man who will only give advice and instruction, and pray fervently to God for the deliverance of the person in question. Many heavy burdens are borne on the shoulders of women who have ungodly husbands, which they cannot speak of before the fellowship. Sometimes married men are under heavy burdens because of their wives, and living in great need of advice and heavenly instructions on how to behave towards them. Sometimes there are young men, passionately tempted and drawn towards maidens either too high or too low in rank for them to marry; and young women, in their turn, groaning with love-sickness, without anyone in whom they could confide their thoughts, or who could help them to bear their burden. In such cases there is often a necessity to lay the matter before a faithful, upright and quiet brother, who will take some part of the burden upon himself, and lay it before the throne of grace until the oppressed man, who revealed his complaints and his wounds, gets relief and quiet from his trouble and trial.

(3) Seek to be as ready as any to contribute, according to your means, to the calls of the fellowship, or any other suitable causes that are put before you. If the church officers are poor men, yet let them show a love toward every good work, for their duty is to lead on before the flock in every example of godliness and charity. As the lives of those who profess religion often have more effect on the spirits of men than do their words, so good advice to others—while we ourselves do just the opposite—is like a thief advising men to be honest, while he persists in his thieving; or a common prostitute counselling girls to be chaste, while she herself continues in her uncleanness. Therefore, it is necessary to give good examples to Christ's flock, and for the stewards to give a lead in this matter, as in other things, according as God has prospered them.

(4) Counsel them constantly not to over-indulge their own flesh. Fasting is one of the special duties of the New Testament, and is very profitable for the mortifying of the body of sin, and for subduing lusts that nothing else but this can subdue; and although neither servants nor the poor can do this whenever they will, yet they can refrain from over-

feeding nature, which will always, when too well nourished, become unruly, for the Holy Spirit has said of Israel of old: 'Jeshurun hath waxed fat, and hath kicked.'

Eating well and drinking freely are a wet nurse to many harmful passions. Paul says that he (for all his grace and success in the gospel) keeps under his body and brings it into subjection; lest having preached to others he himself should be a castaway. And in his Epistle to the Philippians he says of the false teachers: 'whose God is their belly, and whose glory (or their boasting) is in their shame . . .' And of the false prophets it is said, in Ezekiel 34, that they fed themselves and not the flock. And the same charge is made, joyfully, against great Babylon in her fall—namely, that she had 'lived deliciously' with the kings of the earth. And from these various Scriptures we may see that it does not become the professors of religion to be greedy for rich food and strong drink, as says Isaiah the prophet, 'Woe unto them that are mighty to drink wine, and men of strength to mingle strong drink.' And without a doubt such people make gods and idols of their own flesh, and have more respect and care and love for their bellies than for their souls, though the former are to perish and the latter to last for ever. Our Lord says to His Apostles in Luke 21, 'And take heed to yourselves, lest at any time your hearts be overcharged with surfeiting, and drunkenness, and cares of this life, and so that day come upon you unawares.' And if it was necessary for our Lord to warn His apostles to be watchful, who had received the fulness of His Spirit, and moreover lived in days of mockery, persecution and indifference, when one would suppose it was natural to be on guard, how much more necessary for us in these days, when there is no persecution or suffering for preaching the Word, but rather, respect and love towards everyone who speaks a word for God, as for a messenger sent from heaven, together with a too generous preparation of good things, beyond their means by some poor members, and that from a true love for the gospel of Christ, though others are negligent in this matter.

Over-eating and drinking are often followed by astonishingly bad results; scores of sins, lapses, and disgraces have occurred because of gluttony and feasting. How much vain talk? irreverence of spirit? empty jesting? foolish talking? boastful, lustful, quarrelsome thoughts result from this? Yes, and how much breaking of confidences and of taking sides, together with various other fruits of a too self-satisfied and unbroken heart, that an empty stomach or a sober head would never have allowed? Alas! what a loathsome sight, to see religious people, who ought to be delighting in divine food, the body and blood of the Son of Man, yet lusting with such an appetite for the things which feed the mortal body, and seeking for such things, even as the babe seeks its mother's breast. Counsel God's flock to mortify their members which are on the earth; and not to be held captive by a lust for anything whatsoever. It is a pity to see those professing religion wasting so much of their time, and indulging in so much empty talk over their tea or their coffee, or some sweetmeat or other, without spending one-fifth of that time on their knees at their bedside, or on their knees at family prayers either. Alas! how horrible that religious people should find it more to their taste and their enjoyment after the sermon to take snuff, to chew, and to smoke the leaf from the Virginian fields, to pass round the great tankard, to drink deeply of the frothy beer, the sweet wine, the punch, the toddy, or the rum, than to read or meditate, sing or converse about God and His work! You children of the Kingdom, sons of the living God, leave the rum, the brandy, the gin, and the liquor to men who want to fatten their flesh for the worms, though it means losing their souls for all eternity. Warn them diligently about these things, my son, and you will be a worthy overseer to care for God's flock.

(5) Warn them not to be idle, but diligent in their various callings. Remember the word that the Lord spoke to Adam, when He turned him out of the Garden of Eden: 'In the sweat of thy face shalt thou eat bread, till thou return unto the ground; for out of it wast thou taken: for dust thou art, and unto dust shalt thou return' (Gen. 3: 19). And the Apostle Paul says the same thing: 'For yourselves know how ye ought to follow us: for we behaved not ourselves disorderly among you; neither did we eat any man's bread for nought; but wrought with labour and travail night and day, that we might not be chargeable to any of you: not because we have not power, but to make ourselves an ensample unto you to follow us. For even when we were with you, this we commanded you, that if any would not work, neither should he eat. For we hear that there are some which walk among you disorderly, working not at all, but are busybodies. Now them that are such we command and exhort by our Lord Jesus Christ, that with quietness they work, and eat their own bread' (2 Thess. 3: 7-12).

Oh, the sad and wretched results of idleness, which are seen in every age, but most wretched of all when seen in a child of God! David—at other times a man after God's own heart—yet on one occasion, having fallen into a spirit of idleness, looked from the roof of his house upon the wife of Uriah the Hittite, and desired her; and you have seen the miserable consequences that came of that—the sword never more departed from his house. And various consequences, as wretched again, frequently follow from the same cause, namely (besides want and hunger) empty talk, gossiping, spreading lies, increasing bad feeling, revealing secrets, blackening a good name, burdening others, and becoming pompous boasters and useless in the service of God and men. For this reason, Paul speaks to Timothy about widows who desired to be supported by the church: 'But the younger widows refuse: for when they have begun to wax wanton against Christ, they will marry; having damnation, because they have cast off their first faith. And withal they learn to be idle, wandering about from house to house; and not only idle, but tattlers also and busybodies, speaking things which they ought not' (1 Tim. 5: 11-13).

Therefore, my son, counsel the Lord's people to labour, working with their hands the thing which is good, that they may have to give to him that needeth, as the Apostle bids in Ephesians 4: 28; and not only that, but also do your best to give or find work for them, so that there shall be no complaints of an idle spirit in the church of the living God; but rather, that believers should be praised in their callings above all others —religious menservants, maidservants and hired men surpassing all others in faithfulness, honesty, and unfailing diligence, according to their ability and skill; so that the ungodly world are forced to believe, at last, that these excel, not only in chastity, integrity and truthfulness, but also in a proper spirit to do unto others as they would wish others to do unto them; so that they, thus, become the salt of the earth; a sweet savour in the world in every aspect of behaviour, and like lighted candles to the districts in which they live.

And now, my beloved, I am leaving you to the wisdom of heaven, which is able to make you a faithful instructor to weak souls in the midst of their various circumstances and trials, to comfort or to reprove all as the occasion demands. Oh, pray very much to the Father of spirits to lead you in every aspect of this great work, with which there is nothing under the sun to compare for its substance and its glory. The promise which our Lord gave to His Apostles, and not only to them, but also to those who should believe in their words—namely, that He would be with them always, even unto the end of the world—you have a right to claim as your own, and as if it had been given to you alone. Therefore, in the strength of the words of the living God, go forward, and allow nothing to discourage you; you will receive all things that you need, when you ask them for the cause of God; and He has never failed to hear His people's cry when they seek Him with all their heart. Farewell, and may the God of peace bless you and prosper you and strengthen you to promote His glory. Amen.

Lightning Source UK Ltd.
Milton Keynes UK
UKOW04f1925110116

266179UK00001B/267/P